THE TRADITION OF FEMALE TRANSVESTISM IN EARLY MODERN EUROPE

Also by Rudolf M. Dekker and Lotte C. van de Pol
DAAR WAS LAATST EEN MEISJE LOOS

Also by Rudolf M. Dekker
OPROEREN IN HOLLAND GEZIEN DOOR TIJDGENOTEN
HOLLAND IN BEROERING

The Tradition of Female Transvestism in Early Modern Europe

Rudolf M. Dekker
Department of Social History
Erasmus University Rotterdam

and

Lotte C. van de Pol
Department of Social History
Erasmus University Rotterdam

Foreword by Peter Burke
Fellow, Emmanuel College, Cambridge

© Rudolf M. Dekker and Lotte C. van de Pol 1989
Foreword © Peter Burke 1989
Translation by Judy Marcure and Lotte Van de Pol

All rights reserved. No reproduction, copy or transmission of this publication may be made without written permission.

No paragraph of this publication may be reproduced, copied or transmitted save with written permission or in accordance with the provisions of the Copyright Act 1956 (as amended), or under the terms of any licence permitting limited copying issued by the Copyright Licensing Agency, 33–4 Alfred Place, London WC1E 7DP.

Any person who does any unauthorised act in relation to this publication may be liable to criminal prosecution and civil claims for damages.

First published 1989

Published by
THE MACMILLAN PRESS LTD
Houndmills, Basingstoke, Hampshire RG21 2XS
and London
Companies and representatives
throughout the world

Filmsetting by Vantage Photosetting Co Ltd,
Eastleigh and London
Printed in Hong Kong

British Library Cataloguing in Publication Data
Dekker, Rudolf M.
The tradition of female transvestism
in early modern Europe.
1. Transvestism   Netherlands   History
2. Women   Netherlands   Clothing and
dress   History 3. Women   Netherlands
   Sexual behavior   History
I. Title II. Pol, Lotte C. van de
306.7′7   HQ77
ISBN 0-333-41252-4
ISBN 0-333-41253-2 Pbk

To Florence and Ed

Contents

List of Plates	ix
Foreword by Peter Burke	xi
Preface	xiii

1	INTRODUCTION	1
2	WOMEN WHO LIVED AS MEN	5
	Traditional Forms of Temporary Cross-dressing	6
	Women Who Lived as Men: the Data	8
	Their Professions as Men	9
	Origins and Youth	10
	The Transformation	13
	Looks as a Man	16
	The Impersonation	17
	The End of the Disguise	19
3	MOTIVES AND TRADITION	25
	Romantic Motives	27
	Patriotic Motives	30
	Economic Motives	32
	Criminality	35
	The European Tradition of Female Transvestism	39
	Anthropological Findings	41
	Saints and Virgins	44
4	SEXUALITY	47
	The History of Sexuality	47
	Biological Intersexuality	49
	Transvestism	53
	Homosexuality: the Phallocentric View	55
	The Women Who as 'Men' Courted and Married Women	58
	Transsexuality: the Story of Maria van Antwerpen	63
	From Tribades to Lesbians: a Theory	69

5	**CONDEMNATION AND PRAISE**	73
	Legislation and the Bible	75
	Judicial Authorities	76
	Officers in the Fleet and Army	80
	Public Opinion and Popular Songs	82
	Differences between Common Folk and the Elite	90
	Cross-dressing in Literature	92
	Contacts with Royalty	95
	Conclusion	97
6	**SOME CONCLUSIONS**	99

Appendix   104
Notes   113
Index   126

List of Plates

1. Print from c. 1700. Portrait of the Dutch Geertruid ter Brugge, who served as a dragoon in the Dutch army. (Atlas van Stolk 3004, Historische Museum, Rotterdam).
2. Illustration from a book of anecdotes published in Amsterdam in 1659. It depicts a woman discovered on the battlefield in 1589, found killed together with her lover. Both were soldiers in the Dutch army during the Revolt against Spain. (J. H. Glazemaker, *Toneel der wereltsche veranderingen*, Amsterdam, 1659, Universiteitsbibliotheek Amsterdam).
3. Illustration, after a portrait from 1630, of Catalina de Erauso, a Spanish 'conquistador' around 1600. (Catalina de Erauso, *Historia de la Monja Alferez*, Paris, 1829, Universiteitsbibliotheek Amsterdam).
4. Title-page from a play (1739) about Kenau Simons Hasselaar, the sixteenth-century heroine who defended Haarlem against the Spanish enemy. (Universiteitsbibliotheek Amsterdam).
5. Title-page from the biography of 'Claartje', a woman who worked as a stable-boy and coachman for twelve years in Amsterdam. The book was published immediately after her death and subsequent discovery in 1743. The book, however, granted her a happy end, and depicted her alive and married to a rich gentleman. (Universiteitsbibliotheek Amsterdam).
6. Title-page from the Dutch translation of *L'Héroine Mousquetaire* by Jean de Préchac (1679). This is a fictionalised biography of Christine de Meyrak, a French female soldier. (Universiteitsbibliotheek Amsterdam).
7. Illustration from a biography of the French Geneviève Prémoy, who as 'Chevalier Balthazar' was decorated and was admitted in the order of St. Louis by Louis XIV. (*Histoire de la dragoone*, Bruxelles, 1721, Universiteitsbibliotheek Nijmegan).

8 and 9. Anne Bonney and Mary Read, as depicted in the Dutch translation of *A General History of the Pyrates* (1725). (*Historie der Engelsche zeerovers*, Amsterdam 1725, Universiteitsbibliotheek Amsterdam).

10. Title-page and print from the English translation of a biography (1755) of Catharine Vizzani, an Italian female cross-dresser. (British Library, London).

11 and 12. Hannah Snell, as she performed on stage in her male guise. In this way she exploited the publicity following the discovery of her sex. Illustrations from the Dutch translation (1750) of her biography *The Female Soldier*. (*De vrouwelijke soldaat*, Amsterdam, 1725, Universiteitsbibliotheek Amsterdam).

13. Portrait of Hannah Snell in *The Gentleman's Magazine*. (Koninklijke Bibliotheek Den Haag).
14. Illustrations from a ballad published in London at the end of the seventeenth century called *The Female Warrior*, relating how a woman in man's attire obtained an ensign's place. (Left: British Library, London; right: Bodleian Library, Oxford, Douce Ballads 1, 79).
15. A Dutch ballad from c. 1690, which essentially tells the story of Trijn Jurriaens. (*Uytertse hylickmaekers*, Universiteitsbibliotheek Amsterdam).

16. Title-page of the *Kloekmoedige Land- en Zee Heldin* ('The stout-hearted heroine of the land and the sea') (1720) (Universiteitsbibliotheek Amsterdam).
17. During the first three interrogations of her trial in 1769 Maria van Antwerpen insisted that she was a man, and she signed as 'Maggiel van Handtwerpen'. At the fourth interrogation she admitted that she was a woman, and signed as 'Maria van Antwerpen'. (GA Gouda RA 171).
18. Ann Mills, an English female sailor, from the eighteenth century. P. Achroyd, *Dressing up* (London: Thames and Hudson, 1979).
19. 'Mother Ross' who fought around 1700 as an English soldier on Dutch territory. P. Achroyd, *Dressing up* (London: Thames and Hudson, 1979).
20. Illustration from a Dutch biography of the German Antoinette Berg, who fought as a soldier in the English army on Dutch territory in 1799. Afterwards, she served in the British navy in the Caribbean. (Museum des buitengewonen en wondervollen, Amsterdam, 1820, Koninklijke Bibliotheek Den Haag).

21 and 22. Title-page and illustration from the Dutch translation of the memoirs (1815) of the French Renée Bordereau, who fought in the counter-revolutionary army during the French Revolution. (Geschiedenis van Renée Bordereau genoemd Langevin, Dordrecht, 1815, Koninklijke Bibliotheek Den Haag).

23. Illustration from the *Narinnen-spiegel* ('Mirror of female fools'): 'Here the woman wears the man's attire/ and puts on the sword/ yes, seems to defy the man/ but that dolt, afraid of blows/ bears this suffering, and has patience/ what can he do? It is his fault.' (Abraham a St. Clara, *Narinnen-spiegel*, Amsterdam, 1718, Universiteitsbibliotheek, Amsterdam).

24, 25, 26 and 27. Details from Dutch eighteenth-century children's prints with the theme of 'The world turned upside down'.

24, 25 and 26: 'The woman goes to war'.

27: 'The girl, of weak and tender nature/ carried away with arrogance/ here we see in a soldier's uniform/ I think this is foolish. (C. F. van Veen, *Drie eeuwen Noord-nederlandse kinderprenten*, 's Gravenhage, 1971, Universiteitsbibliotheek Amsterdam).

28. Painted canvas used by a nineteenth-century German streetsinger, illustrating a song about a female soldier in the American Civil War. The theme is the ancient one of a woman who dressed as a man to follow her lover into the army and dies together with him on the battlefield (compare ill. no. 2). (Museum für Deutsche Volkskunde, W. Berlin).

Foreword

At first sight female cross-dressing, the subject of this book, may appear to be somewhat marginal, one of the byways of history. Appearances, however, are often misleading. The study of belief in the curative power of the 'royal touch', published in 1923 by the great French historian Marc Bloch, was dismissed by an English colleague as 'this curious bypath of yours'. All the same, this bypath turned out to be a main road leading to a new kind of history, the history of mentalities. In a similar way, this new book by Rudolf Dekker and Lotte van de Pol has its place in the development of a new kind of social history, a development which is taking place in a number of centres which include Paris and Princeton, Cambridge and Bologna, the Max Planck Institute at Göttingen and the Department of Social History in the Erasmus University of Rotterdam, to which the two authors of this book belong.

Social history is not exactly a new subject: the 'history of society' was already being written in the eighteenth century in France, Scotland, Italy, the Netherlands and elsewhere. It has, however, taken a new turn in the last fifteen or twenty years. Social historians have become concerned with the view 'from below' as well as from above, and with the history of women as well as men. Rudolf Dekker, for example, has published a book about riots and revolts in Dutch towns, while Lotte van de Pol has been working on the history of prostitution in Amsterdam. In this study, the list of 119 'women living as men' in the Netherlands between 1550 and 1839 is a fascinating piece of historical detection in itself, and it is to be hoped that historians of other countries where women joined the army or the navy (For example, England, Russia and Brazil) will be inspired to emulate it. As for the authors' psychological and social interpretations of the phenomenon, they should appeal to anyone interested in the everyday life of ordinary women – and men – in Europe before the French and Industrial Revolutions. In the course of their investigation, the authors throw a good deal of light on the history of poverty, the history of crime, and the history of sexuality.

Another significant change in the social history written in the last fifteen or twenty years – for example, by Natalie Davis, by Carlo Ginzburg, by Emmanuel Le Roy Ladurie, by Keith Thomas, by Edward Thompson – is its 'anthropological turn'. Rudolf Dekker and Lotte van de Pol have not described their book as a study in 'historical anthropology', but they have drawn on recent work by anthropologists on cross-dressing in Asian, African and American societies, the better to understand the European tradition. Their study also addresses a question which is of increasing concern to anthropologists, sociologists and historians alike; the question of identity. A generation ago, the emphasis was on so-called 'objective' factors; the description of social structure, the measurement of social trends, the analysis of social functions. Nowadays, in contrast, the stress falls on the different ways in which people perceive and interpret their own society, and in the process 'construct' the social reality in which they live. Perceptions of self and perceptions of the 'other', against whom the self is defined, have become central to anthropological, sociological and historical studies. There is, for example, great interest in 'ethnicity' and in the process of creating national identity.

Gender, however, like social class, is only just beginning to be studied in this way, so that Rudolf Dekker and Lotte van de Pol are carrying out the work of pioneers. Their investigation into women who dressed as men and joined the army or navy takes them into the world of ballads and folktales (not to mention hagiography), and raises fascinating questions about the interaction between social 'reality' and literature (or myth). The authors make good use of the autobiographies of a few of their heroines, from the vivid and moving self-portrait of Maria van Antwerpen to the account of 'Hendrik van de Berg', on the border between autobiography and fiction as well as between male and female roles, neither one thing nor the other. This study of 119 cases of women who broke some of the most fundamental unwritten rules of their culture, tells us something important about the nature of that culture and also about the process by which each one of us constructs a social identity.

PETER BURKE

Preface

Our curiosity roused by a few chance findings of female cross-dressers, we started to collect cases systematically in 1979 as a by-product of our more regular historical research. This resulted in the book *Daar was laatst een meisje loos: Nederlandse vrouwen als matrozen en soldaten*, published by Ambo in 1981. The offer from Macmillan to publish an English translation of the Dutch book made us renew our investigations. From September 1985 to September 1986 we rewrote the text completely and the result turned out not to be a translation but a new and different book. Many people contributed to both the Dutch and the English version. Cross-dressing or transvestism is a subject which can only be researched systematically to a limited extent and we owe many references to historians, archivists and others who knew we were looking for information on this subject. Among those we want to thank are C. R. Boxer, J. R. Bruyn, Peter Burke, Herman Diederiks, Bas Dudok van Heel, Florike Egmond, Petronella Elema, Els van Eyck van Heslinga, Sjoerd Faber, Eco Haitsma Mulier, Gert Hekma, Arend Huussen, Gert Jan Johannes, Jean Jüngen, Maria Leuker, Theo van der Meer, C. F. L. Paul, Joke Spaans, and Pieter Spierenburg. And, of course, without the help of librarians and archivists a work like this is not possible.

René Grémaux let us read his dissertation in progress on 'sworn virgins' in the Balkans and we profited much from the discussions we had. Anna Clark and Julie Wheelwright shared their work in progress on female cross-dressers in England with us. Estelle Cohen and Ivan Gaskell in England, Andrea Michler in France, and Wayne Tebrake in the United States helped us in finding books which were not available in the Netherlands. We also want to thank the Department of History of the Erasmus University at Rotterdam for the facilities offered and our colleagues for their support. Anton Blok, Florike Egmond, Theo van der Meer and Pieter Spierenburg commented on earlier versions or parts of it, much to the benefit of the book. We profited from presenting and discussing our ideas on transsexuality and Maria van Antwerpen at the conference 'Sexualiteit in de Achttiende Eeuw', 13–15 September 1984, at Gent. We are also grateful to Jean-Louis

Flandrin for giving us the opportunity to discuss our ideas at his seminar at the Ecole des Hautes Etudes en Sciences Sociales at Paris, 21 March 1986. The lively discussions there certainly made us reconsider some of our ideas.

Judy Marcure translated most of the drafts and corrected the final text, giving her last comments even on the eve of her emigration to Australia. We want to thank her for her enthusiasm and support. We are also grateful to the Netherlands Organisation for the Advancement of Pure Research (ZWO) for subsidising part of the translation.

Finally our greatest debts are to Florence Koorn and Ed Elbers who gave us, over the years, ample moral and practical support. They also, from their own disciplines as a historian and a psychologist respectively, suggested much literature and discussed many ideas with us. Therefore we dedicate this book to both of them.

RUDOLF M. DEKKER
LOTTE C. VAN DE POL

I spoke to you of Amazons before . . . but I could give you many examples of women on our own ships who did men's service and were exceptionally brave. Of these I could tell many amusing stories only they would take up too much paper. I could also tell you how I myself have discovered women in soldier's clothing in our armies and made them change their dress. During my days in the army a girl in the cavalry was caught plundering and suffered herself to be hung without making her sex known. This the sergeant on duty told me; he had her undressed after she had died and felt sorry about it. And are such women not also Amazons?

Nicolaas Witsen
Amsterdam statesman and amateur geographer, 1641–1717
(J. F. Gebhart, *Het leven van mr. Nicolaas Cornelisz. Witsen,* Utrecht, 1882, II, p. 408)

1
Introduction

On 23 February in the year 1769, a woman was condemned by the court of the Dutch city of Gouda for 'gross and excessive fraud in changing her name and quality' and 'mocking holy and human laws concerning marriage'. Her crime was that she had eight years before dressed herself in men's clothing, given herself a man's name, and had enlisted as a soldier. Worse, in this disguise she had courted and married another woman. Moreover, in 1751 she had been tried for exactly the same offences.

The story of Maria van Antwerpen, as this woman was christened, generated some sensation in her own time. In later centuries she would sometimes be found among the footnotes of military history, where her story was presented as a curious, amusing incident. But however fascinating the story is, we are interested in it for more than its anecdotal value. The difference between a male and a female is the primary and most essential differentiation made in society. The notion that one is male or female is formed very early in infancy and is the most deeply rooted aspect of our identities. A 'change of sex' is therefore a very dramatic decision.

What is more, Maria van Antwerpen was in her time not so exceptional as she would have been in ours. During extensive, but by its very nature not systematic, research we collected 119 cases of women living as men in the history of the Netherlands, nearly all of them from the seventeenth and eighteenth centuries.[1] More superficial research showed that female cross-dressers were not only to be found in the Dutch Republic. From Denmark in the north to Spain and Italy in the south, there were examples of such women.[2] However, only in England did we find a quantity of cases comparable with Holland. A far-from-exhaustive investigation into the literature resulted in fifty authentic cases of female transvestism in the seventeenth and eighteenth centuries in Great Britain.[3]

In this book we argue that such women should not be categorised as incidental human curiosities, but that their cross-dressing was part of a deeply rooted tradition. In the early modern era passing oneself off as a man was a real and viable option for women who had fallen into bad times and were struggling to overcome their difficult circumstances. This tradition existed throughout Europe, but was strongest by far in the north-west, in the Netherlands, England and Germany. We will also argue that the pressures which led to the decision of cross-dressing could be both material, such as poverty, or emotional, such as a patriotic fervour or love for another woman, or a combination of these.

This tradition of female cross-dressing may have had its roots in medieval times, but it became visible in the late sixteenth century; it was lost in the nineteenth century. Traces of this are very limited nowadays; in Holland, we find them only in a popular children's song, *Daar was laatst een meisje loos*, which begins in the following way:

> There once was a maiden gay*
> Who wished to sail
> Who wished to sail
> There once was a maiden gay
> Who wished as a sailor to sail away.
> **'loos' in Dutch also means naughty, cunning

In the following lines she enlists for seven years, but when she fails to hoist the sails properly, she escapes punishment by revealing herself to be a girl and offering herself as the captain's mistress. This song goes back to at least the eighteenth century, when it was certainly not a children's song, but a sailor's working song, to be sung as the sails were being hoisted.[4]

We found many more popular songs with this theme in the seventeenth and eighteenth centuries, not only in Holland but all over Europe. Moreover, female cross-dressers appeared in novels, in fictionalised biographies and memoirs, in prints, and in plays and operas. The prominence of the theme in literature in the seventeenth and eighteenth centuries must have fed upon and shaped the reality of female transvestism to some extent, but as a literary theme it had its own tradition and clichés.

We decided to study the reality rather than the image of female cross-dressing, and will concentrate on the documented Dutch cases. We found these women in all sorts of printed and archival material, but our best sources turned out to be judicial archives and the archives of the VOC (*Verenigde Oostindische Compagnie*= the Dutch East India Company). Newspapers, chronicals, medical treatises, collections of anecdotes and travel reports also yielded cases. No archives of the time, however, had entries or headings that could be looked through systematically for cross-dressers. Only those judicial archives that had been made accessible before have been researched in their totality. Chance findings of our own and of fellow historians added to our list considerably.

Many archives have been lost and many others have not been researched. Moreover, we do not know how many cross-dressers left no trail behind them in written source-material. We can make a guess that this especially concerns those women who transformed themselves so successfully that they were never unmasked. For these reasons, we presume that our 119 cases are only the tip of the iceberg. For the same reasons, it is impossible to know how representative they are, and we can only guess that there is an overrepresentation of failure, and of women on ships where it was most difficult of all to hide one's real identity.

In spite of this, it was possible to sketch a coherent image of the women concerned. We could see clear lines and patterns that fitted most of these cases of cross-dressing. The practical problems, for example, were the same for all the women; we noted a number of similarities in motives, and equally so in the reactions to this phenomenon by the women's contemporaries. Above all, it was clear that these were not incidental cases, but that they were part of a tradition of cross-dressing of which they were well aware.

In Chapter 2 we will first give a description of the background of these women, of how they impersonated men and how they were discovered to be women. In Chapter 3, we will try to reconstruct what motives each of them had personally and how these fitted in with the general tradition of female transvestism. Chapter 4 is devoted to sexual aspects, discussing if biological or sexual incentives for it can be found. In Chapter 5, we will explore the reactions of the contemporaries to the phenomenon.

But before going into these questions, we want to return to Maria van Antwerpen, our best documented case, to discuss some methodological problems.[5] Maria van Antwerpen was born in the garrison town Breda in 1719. She was an orphan at twelve, and worked as a maidservant with different employers. In 1746, she enlisted as a soldier under the name of 'Jan van Ant', and a year later officially married a woman who was not aware of her true sex. When her army unit was billeted in Breda, in 1751, Maria was recognised and discovered.

Her arrest caused a great deal of commotion: the news appeared in the press, a song was written and sung about her, and even before she was sentenced an autobiography appeared, named *De Bredasche Heldinne* ('The Heroine of Breda'). This book was written by Franciscus Lievens Kersteman. According to the book's introduction, 'The Heroine of Breda' was based entirely upon Maria's own words. It was common practice in the eighteenth century to chose the form of an autobiography as packaging for a primarily fictional story, but in this case we do believe the author. The sources confirm Kersteman's claim that he served in Maria's army unit at the time, and we could verify most details of names, places, dates and army movements. We feel justified in considering 'The Heroine of Breda' as a journalistic autobiography, with Kersteman as 'ghost writer'.

After her sentence of exile Maria went to live in Gouda, where a few years later a woman persuaded her to live as a man again, in order to marry her. This marriage took place in 1762, and Maria also enlisted as a soldier again. This time her military career was short-lived, but 'Machiel van Antwerpen' continued pretending to be a man, a husband and even a father, until a visit to Gouda in 1769 brought recognition and arrest. The 5 consecutive hearings, in which she was intensively interrogated, resulted in 43 folio pages of text. The court also asked for information in other towns, so that these interrogations form an important source, confirming and supplementing much of what she told Kersteman in 1751. Maria was banished again, and the only thing we know of her further life is that she died in Breda in 1781.

It should be clear from the above that the life of Maria van Antwerpen is unusually well documented – far better, in fact, than that of other women from the common people in the eighteenth century or before. Cases of cross-dressing drew most attention when the disguised women courted or married other women. The extensive documentation of these was supplemented quantitatively with other, less spectacular cases: together this formed the firm foundation upon which to build this study of women who went through life as men in the seventeenth and eighteenth centuries.

2
Women Who Lived as Men

While I was detained in Amsterdam, I made by chance the acquaintance of a certain Willempje Gerrits of Emden, who had recently fought in the battle of Funen in Denmark, dressed in male attire; there, she had behaved herself so valiantly, according to the witness of the menfolk present at this battle with her, that she served as an example to others. This maid earned her bed and board by doing scullery work, or if she found no work of this kind, with spinning, but this was so against her spirit, that she repeatedly professed a fierce passion for war and only waited for a propitious moment to surrender once again to that bloody trade. Because I thought I could choose no better companion, I went to her house, where I found her seated at the spinning wheel. 'How sorry a sight', I said, 'to see you sitting here and spinning, while the drum is being beaten! Hurl the wheel into the fire and go into service again!.' As I spoke these words to her, I saw a small axe which was used to cut peat whereupon I so dispatched the household devil, that it could never again be used by anyone. 'What is to be done now?' said Willempje, 'you have hewn the wheel into pieces, but I have no money to buy men's clothing, without which you know I can never be taken on.' 'That is a small scruple,' I said, 'I have still enough money to buy an old suit and once we have that, we shall sell this woman's garb and we shall get enough of it to get another old suit for you, and then we shall be ready.'

Willempje found this suggestion so to her taste that we directly set out for the Noordermarkt where we quickly achieved our aims because we cared little if the garments were a trifle torn or patched, so long as we appeared to be men in them. We then bought English caps for us both, in exchange for a skirt belonging to Willempje, and each cut the hair of the other just below the ears, and we applied ourselves to the office of the Admiralty at the Prinsenhof.[1]

These lines come from an autobiography of one 'Hendrik van de Berg', which tells 'his' adventures as a soldier first and then a sailor in the 1660s and 1670s. The book appeared anonymously, and 'Hendrik's' name as a woman we are not told. We do not know if 'Hendrik' was a historical person; but Willempje Gerrits certainly was. The names and military details in her story are accurate, and the descriptions of military life ring very true to life. The 'Stout-Hearted Heroine of the Land and the Sea', as the book is titled, can be an authentic autobiography, but may also be a work of fiction, strewn with historical facts, by an author who knew the world he was describing very well. But whatever its nature, it contains some of the most colourful and detailed descriptions of women who chose to live as men that we have found. In the fragment above, this is the moment when the heroine's decision to change her sex was made, culminating in the destruction of the symbol of women's work and women's place, the spinning wheel, and her assumption of the masculine counterpart, the accoutrements of military life.

In this chapter we will try to reconstruct the lives of the women who impersonated men: where they came from, their backgrounds, what professions they chose, what they looked like, how they succeeded and how they failed. Of course, many of these questions can only be answered tentatively. In many cases, especially when women were discovered on ships, we know little more than a name, a birthplace and their male profession. Yet these cases may well constitute the most typical of those encountered. The cases that yield the most details, on the other hand, could well be the most atypical: for example, those in which a cross-dressing woman married another woman, which usually led to extensive judicial interrogations.

TRADITIONAL FORMS OF TEMPORARY CROSS-DRESSING

In the early modern period there were several occasions where it was customary and sometimes even acceptable for women to dress as a man for a short time. The main examples of this are transvestism during carnival festivities, during riots, while travelling or in flight, for the sake of erotic stimulation or carousing. We have excluded cases like these from our list, as the disguise was for a very short time only and was sometimes easy to see through, or even meant to be seen through. Still, these forms of cross-dressing were common. 'The world turned upside down' was a powerful image in pre-industrial Europe, and the knowledge of these traditions must have made the idea of long-term transvestism more conceivable.[2] And one type could lead to the other. We know of several instances in which a carnival provided the stimulus for more permanent cross-dressing, or where temporary cross-dressing for the purpose of a flight or a journey was the beginning of a life in men's clothing.

Cross-dressing – and of course, dressing up in general – was always among the customs surrounding carnival. This festivity was forbidden in the Dutch Republic as 'papish superstition', but it took a long time before it was repressed and remnants continued to manifest themselves in other festivities. This connection is apparent in one case in 1659, in which a woman in Amsterdam started dressing herself as a man in the second half of February, arguing that it could easily pass as one of the activities surrounding Shrove Tuesday. Demonstrations and riots were also linked to a tradition of transvestism, and the borderline between a festivity and a riot could become blurred. At a big celebration in honour of the wedding of an Amsterdam fishwife in 1784, one of the women participants took the role of a man, wig and all. Eventually, this party turned into a political demonstration in support of the Prince of Orange.[3] During an Orangist demonstration in The Hague in 1747, a woman dressed 'in Amazon garb, with a grenadier's cap of orange paper on her head'.[4] And during a riot in 1787 in Gorinchem, during which several houses were plundered, one of the leaders of the crowd was a woman in men's clothing.[5]

Cross-dressing for fun can be found in all social strata. In the middle of the seventeenth century, the daughter of the Clerk of the Estates General occasionally donned men's clothing and joined a group of young men who amused themselves by making the streets of The Hague unsafe.[6] Two maidservants in the household of a Delft regent amused themselves in a similar way in 1694. One of them donned the clothing of her master, his trousers, his stockings and his shoes, finishing her costume by placing his fur hat on her head. The other dressed in her mistress's clothes, pretending to be 'his' wife. Elegantly attired in this way, they went to a nearby village where they visited friends, then to a waffle stall, and finally to an inn, where they hired a violinist to play for them, dancing until late into the night.[7]

There were also women who occasionally donned men's clothing for erotic stimulation. An Amsterdam prostitute received her clients dressed as a Persian boy.[8] That this type of cross-dressing was regarded as erotic is confirmed in the diary of Constantijn Huygens Jr, who described how an acquaintance was approached by a procuress who offered him a young manservant. Upon closer inspection, the latter turned out to be a young girl in men's clothing.[9] Most of these cases were mere incidents, like the visit to an Amsterdam brothel by a man and a woman who had dressed in men's clothing.[10]

There are many examples of women who dressed as men for travelling. This was considered a safety precaution, particularly for longer trips because a woman travelling alone, faced considerable danger in a time where highway robbers still were common in Europe. Masculine attire was also more practical for travel than long skirts. Maria Anna Steinhaus, a courtesan who enticed a chamberlain of the Prince of Orange into marrying her, usually travelled and even went hunting in men's clothing. When her husband went bankrupt, this male disguise proved very handy for eluding creditors.[11] Steinhaus, a German woman by birth, had been a dancer at the Italian comedy in Paris before her marriage. Her former profession and her predeliction for cross-dressing were certainly not unrelated. Trouser-roles for women were very popular in plays and opera at the time, even in the street-theatre.[12] Several actresses preferred male clothing in real life too. A Dutch example is the eighteenth-century actress Mietje de Bruin, who specialised in performing male roles and often dressed in men's clothes off stage, especially when going out at night.[13]

WOMEN WHO LIVED AS MEN: THE DATA

The cases upon which the following descriptions are based consist of women who for a considerable time lived as men in every perceivable external aspect, or whom we judge to have had the intention to do so, even if they were quickly discovered to be women. The difference from temporary masquerades was not always clear, however, and some decisions must remain arbitrary. Even within our list of 'permanent' cross-dressers, only a minority probably had in mind that this was for the rest of their lives. In these hundred or so cases there were different kinds of cross-dressing, varying in duration, intentions and motives.

We began by trying to establish what they had in common, and we found that their backgrounds, the ways in which they transformed themselves, and the ways in which they ended their male careers showed many similarities. It is in the first place remarkable that the cases are distributed rather evenly in time, with the exception of periods of war when more female soldiers and sailors were always found, and that the pattern did not really change in the course of the seventeenth and eighteenth centuries. The phenomenon appeared rather suddenly at the end of the sixteenth century. In the largest Dutch city, Amsterdam, only one case was found for the whole of that century. This is no distortion of the sources as the judicial archives of this city for the sixteenth century have been well conserved and the criminal sentences were researched in their totalities. During the seventeenth and eighteenth centuries, this city produced many of our women, whereas the criminal series have only partially been researched. The only example where we studied the complete series of sentences, Leiden 1533–1811, did not show a case of female cross-dressing before 1606. Then, at the beginning of the nineteenth century, the number of cases dwindles sharply and the phenomenon disappears as suddenly as it had appeared.

For nearly all the women we know how they earned their living as men, and in about half of the cases their age and birthplace is known to us. All other information, although extensive in some cases, is incidental. Especially concerning the reasons for their transvestism, their early years, and their feelings in general, information is scarce. Still, what we know forms a sufficiently coherent picture to justify our drawing some general conclusions.

THEIR PROFESSIONS AS MEN

Of the 93 women we know had their professions as men, eighty-three were – or had at one time been – sailors or soldiers. Many of the soldiers were marines or were transported overseas to serve with the East or West India Company; a minority served with the navy. So more than half of the disguised women practised a trade at sea – precisely where, in fact, the chance of discovery was greatest. Privacy was at a minimum on ships and one lived for extended periods of time with the same group of about 150 to 400 men in a crowded forecastle. This relatively great risk of discovery may have led to an overrepresentation of seafaring women, but even so this apparent preference for the sea must be a real one, if only because young unschooled lower-class 'men' had few other alternatives from which to choose careers.

The land army harboured 22 of our women. This probably is an underestimation because it was easier to hide one's real identity in the army than at sea, as is indicated by the fact that two-thirds of our known land soldiers had been in service for extended periods of time. Only a few of the women on ships were able to continue their disguise for more than a few months.

A stable civilian's life on shore offered the best possibility to hide a female identity. We know of a few women who worked as a journeyman, silk-winder, pipemaker, stable boy or valet. Most of these were discovered under extreme circumstances, such as the examination of the body after death, or not discovered in this disguise at all. Trijntje Simons, for example, was first a shoemaker, then a stonemason, and finally a soldier. As a soldier she died, and only then her sex was discovered. A substantial number of the disguised civilian women, however, cannot be said to have had any regular profession, living instead on the margins of society, begging, stealing and cheating. Their cross-dressing often was discovered when they were apprehended for their criminal activities.

ORIGINS AND YOUTH

It is a striking and significant fact that so many of our women were born outside the Dutch Republic. Of the 55 women whose birthplace we know, 24 were born beyond the borders of the Republic. Most of these foreigners came from German harbour cities, like Hamburg and Bremen, and from Westphalia. This reflects the general pattern of immigration to the Dutch Republic. The relative prosperity of the country, especially of the cities in the province of Holland, lured many foreigners to the North Sea shores. Before 1650 most of the immigrants came from the Southern Netherlands, and thereafter from Germany and Scandinavia. Male immigrants usually ended up with the fleet, in the army, or doing the least attractive jobs on shore. Large numbers of women also left independently for Holland: their goal was usually to go into domestic service, but many of them ended up in the textile trades or in doing other kinds of lower-class women's work.

In any sample of Dutch lower-class women a substantial number of foreign-born women may be expected, but their representation among the female cross-dressers is disproportionately high, suggesting that being far from home was an element which in many cases contributed to the decision to begin living as a man.[14]

As far as we know, practically all our disguised women came from the lower classes. The number of cases for which we could determine the family background was relatively small, but these stories are remarkably alike. Most of these were orphans or they had lost one parent, and several had had family problems in their youth. One girl, Francina Gunningh, was born out of wedlock and was raised by her grandparents until she was seven years old.[15]

The youth of Maria van Antwerpen is a good example. She was the daughter of a distiller of brandy from Breda. Burdened by a large family, her father became impoverished and finally had to earn a living as a dockworker. Maria lost her mother when she was eleven, and her father when she was twelve years old. Even before that, she was taken in by an aunt, with whom she was very unhappy. Forty years later she still bitterly complained that she was 'mistreated by her aunt', and that she 'did not have the life of a dog, much less that of a child'. As soon as she could, she tried to find a place as a serving girl, but when she was dismissed, she did not dare trust her family for help, deciding instead to become a soldier.

A similar youth and background was found for Maritgen Jans a century earlier. Her father was a gunsmith. He died young, and her mother, a midwife, remarried a schoolmaster. Shortly thereafter, her mother also died, and Maritgen moved in with a married sister. Maritgen was herself betrothed at a very young age, but the marriage never took place. When she was fifteen, she fled to Amsterdam to see if she could build a better life for herself there. Like Maria van Antwerpen, she stated before the court that when she was confronted with imminent poverty, she decided to dress as a man because she did not dare go back to her family.

Barbara Adriaens testified to a court of law in Amsterdam that she had been placed in a house of correction for two years by her family when she was thirteen years old because she had been 'drinking for three days in succession in bad company'. She also told the court that she had once had a quarrel with her brother about money, during which he seriously wounded her. Anna Jans, daughter of a ship's pilot from Texel, said that she decided to disguise herself in men's clothing after a quarrel with her stepmother.

Two of the women on our list told the court that they were born in Oldenburg, Germany, around the middle of the eighteenth century. Margareta Reymers, a peasant's daughter, left for the Netherlands because she was ill-treated at home. Marytje van den Hove was a soldier's daughter. She was four or five years old when her mother died. Then she had to beg for her food in the countryside usually wearing boys' clothes given to her by her brother. Very early in her career as a vagabond she went to the Netherlands.

Most of the stories above were told by the women during their trials, and to some degree can be considered as an attempt to vindicate their cross-dressing. But even if exaggerated, these stories suggest that many of the women had been orphaned or had lost a parent and that they had left their families after conflicts, which surely must have played a role in their choosing such unusual lifestyles. On the other hand, such a background was not at all exceptional in these times. As a result of the tendency to marry late and the fact that average life expectancy was low in pre-industrial Europe many children lost one or both parents early. The remaining parent, certainly if this was the father, tried to remarry quickly, because the division of labour within the household was strongly sex-linked. The wicked stepmother described in folktales could easily have been a reality for many children in pre-industrial times. Also women married generally in their middle twenties, often long after having left their parents' homes to make their own living. Many of them emigrated to other regions or towns: these young women risked finding themselves one day destitute, alone, friendless and disoriented far from home.

Children from the common people were brought into the labour process at an early age, so that most of our women had already had a career of female labour behind them before they tried their luck as men. The information we have on this point suggests that their trades did not differ from those of other women of their class. Typically, as women, our cross-dressers had been servants, seamstresses, twine makers, sheet burlers, knitters or street peddlars: all forms of women's work, characterised by a low degree of schooling, limited prospects and poor pay. In this they did not differ from their normal female contemporaries; however, some stories we know suggest that they were not very successful in their female careers.

It should come as no surprise that the women who abandoned

their own sex and donned men's clothing were nearly always unmarried or were for all practical purposes single. However, there were a few women whom we know to have been married, and their transvestism was directly related to the marital state: they put on men's clothes either to be able to stay with their husbands, or to escape them. We shall say more about this in the next chapter.

THE TRANSFORMATION

Most women were between sixteen and twenty-five years old at the moment they decided to change their sex; that is, their ages ranged from puberty to the age where a woman was legally of age and could expect to be married. In these ten years of adolescence, women of the lower classes generally had to look after themselves, to earn their own living, and, ideally, to accumulate a dowry.

The decision to go through life as a man was followed by serious practical problems. Secrecy was one of the conditions for success, and that meant that the transformation should preferably not be undertaken in a known environment where, despite the disguise, one ran a considerable risk of being recognised. As we have seen, however, many of these women were not in a home environment to begin with. Still, in the interests of anonymity, it might be an advantage to go to yet another place. Barbara Adriaens, who had been a servant in Delft, said she 'sold her women's clothing in Utrecht and bought men's clothing in place of it', and that she 'first cut off her plaits and then went to a barber in a village outside of Utrecht'. Maritgen Jans, who lived in Amsterdam, 'went in the evening to Utrecht, and there, behind a church, took off her women's garments and donned a man's habit, shore off her hair, set a hat on her head, gathered her clothing together, and in an unknown lodging house gave her name as David Jans'.

The common people of the time possessed few clothes, and much of their wardrobe was second-hand: buying and selling at second-hand shops were common. For some women it was necessary to sell first a part of their women's clothing before it was possible to purchase the men's clothing, as it was impossible to discard their female attire openly at a second-hand shop and exchange it then and there for men's clothing. Maria van Spanjen solved this problem by stealing various parts of her new masculine wardrobe at the lodging where she was staying, and so, disguised, fleeing before daybreak, leaving the other guests to look in vain for socks, trousers, shirts, underwear and a hat. A number of women had accomplices who helped them achieve their transformation. Lena Wasmoet, for example, was helped in Amsterdam by another woman who bought men's clothing from a Jew. She passed them to Lena who put them on in a public toilet. In a few cases, two disguised women were discovered on board a single ship and it is not unlikely that they had undertaken the adventure together. The description by the 'Stout-Hearted Heroine' at the beginning of this chapter could very well be historically correct.

These accomplices might also have been the instigators of, or interested parties in, the transformation. At her trial, Vrouwtje Frans told the court that 'a manservant, who was to sail to the East Indies, brought her to this end; he also provided her with the clothing'. This manservant may have been, or may have hoped to become, her lover, a scenario frequently described in popular songs.

There were certainly women and men who earned money by recruiting women for the army or navy. Maria van der Gijsse was made drunk by a woman who afterwards made her sign a contract to go into service as a soldier. Anna Spiesen also said that everything was arranged by another woman, who even made sure that a man registered in her place when the articles were signed. In one case dating from 1644, an army sergeant organised the masquerade. With the help of a soldier, he had persuaded two women to act as soldiers during an inspection of the troops. This seems to have occurred more often.

After changing from female to male, it was of course necessary to take a man's name. Many women chose the male version of their own name, or a male first name taken together with the old patronym or last name: Jacoba Jacobs became 'Jacob' Jacobs, Barbara Adriaens, 'Willem' Adriaens, Annetje Barents, 'Klaas' Barents, Maria van der Gijsse, 'Claes' van der Gijsse, and so on. Other women clung to their father's name, like Trijntje Sijmons, who called herself 'Sijmon Poort'. Maria van Antwerpen tells in her autobiography that she deliberately chose her father's first name, Jan. But perhaps the most striking case is that of Marytje van den Hove, who took on her paternal grandfather's name, Alemondus, thus, according to name-giving customs in this part of Europe, declaring herself symbolically to be her father's son.

At the age at which these women took on the lives of men,

averaging about 20 years, they would have been fully developed physically. The style for men's clothes in the seventeenth and eighteenth centuries of wide jackets and large hats or caps could have hidden a great deal, but would not solve all the problems of the disguise. Nothing could change their smooth chins and high voices, for example. This meant that they were likely to resemble boys rather than men. Fortunately for them, the age at which one began to participate in adult life was younger than it is now. A boy could enter the fleet or the army as early as his fourteenth year. In general, a woman dressed as a man looks younger than her years. Maritgen Jans was among those who discovered this, when, despite her 16 years, she was refused as being too young to become a soldier. Many female cross-dressers were able to blend inconspicuously with the large group of adolescents that would be found on any ship, with any army unit, or in any workshop, and could probably have continued impersonating boys of 16 or so for some time. In fact, Maria van Antwerpen managed to enlist as a boy of 16 when she was 28, and as a young man of 23 when she was in reality already 42 years old.

We encountered few details regarding how these women solved the more intimate physical problems they confronted. Our sources give no indication whatsoever of how they hid and dealt with their menstruation, which must have been difficult in a crowded forecastle or barracks. Moreover not only the presence of feminine, but certainly also the absence of masculine, sex organs could pose problems. One might try to keep one's clothing on continually, but this could eventually raise suspicions, as Marritgen Jans found when she refused to disrobe under the hot African sun. 'Sometimes he went to bathe with the soldiers in a small river, but because he said that he could not swim he kept his shirt and kilt on and did not go further into the water than his calves.' The account told further how '"he" sometimes visited a beautiful negress in order to remove all suspicion from her person'. This, however, was not enough: precisely her refusal to join in public love-making, roused 'wicked suspicions of doing something not befitting virtue . . .'.

A rare reference to this subject is found in the case of Geertruid van den Heuvel, who had 'covered her shameful parts with a leather thong with a copper clasp' by which she more closely resembled a man in that essential spot. But then, she was a corporal of the militia at the beginning of the nineteenth century, when male fashion prescribed extremely narow trousers. There are one or two hints that some women provided themselves with some sort of artificial penis. The most detailed information we have on this point concerns a German case, Catharina Lincken, who was tried in 1721. She succeeded in passing for a man even in her married life, as she made use of 'a leather-covered horn through which she urinated and [which she kept] fastened against her nude body'.[16] In one of the versions of the story of the English female soldier Christian Davies, a 'silver tube' as a urinary device is mentioned, an instrument she was said to have obtained from another female soldier.[17] A similar device is mentioned in a Dutch popular song about a female VOC sailor:

> She pissed through a horn pipe
> Just as a young man might.[18]

Maria van Antwerpen may have alluded to such a design in her autobiography. Soldiers used to sleep two or more to a bed. Maria writes that she feared the physical contact with various young sleeping companions, and that she therefore sometimes kept her trousers on at night. She also provided herself 'with a certain precaution about which chastity forbids me to tell', as she rather mysteriously stated.

LOOKS AS A MAN

The portraits that exist of women dressed as men are not really helpful in giving an impression of how they looked. These are generally illustrations in books or commercial prints, and the figures depicted were meant to be recognised as women in disguise. In literature, these women are usually represented as handsome and charming young men, objects of passion to the women they met. The historical sources, however, do not depict our women as being pretty as women, although as men their charms were usually rated higher. Margaritha Reymers was described by a contemporary as 'large and coarse of body, by which she could easily appear to be a man in her soldier's clothing'. Maritgen Jans was said to be 'too sweet of face to be a man'. But after her discovery, when she again wore women's clothing, it was 'the feeling of many that men's habit became her better'. In her memoirs, Maria van Antwerpen tells how, as a woman, she was 'exceptionally stout', and had the manner of a dragoon. But after she had dressed as a man she looked in a mirror, remarking with satisfaction that she was a handsome boy. In her autobiography she told how a Lieutenant-General fancied her and promoted her in the army, because he 'took pleasure in my free, candid nature and handsome stature.' This detail found its way into the ballad of Maria's life:

> A pearl, she stood there
> Before her captain's stare,
> And he thought he could swear
> He ne'er seen a lad so fair.

THE IMPERSONATION

For all these women in men's clothing, the stress caused by the fear of discovery must have been constant. Of those who succeeded in impersonating men for a considerable period of time, we can easily assume that they possessed strong nerves, some intelligence, and possibly a talent for acting.

The difficulties involved in playing a man's role convincingly and continuously were not restricted to outward appearances. We may suppose that there were adjustment difficulties on the psychological levels as well. There are innumerable differences between men and women, for example in language, mimicry, gestures, carriage, so a change of gender involves more than simply dressing in men's clothing. In general, the women came from the same strata of the population as their male companions, but even within one social group, men's and women's cultures would differ greatly. A passage in Maria van Antwerpen's autobiography indicates that the male approach to sexual matters, certainly within the male worlds of soldiers and seamen, must have seemed brutal to the disguised women. Maria wrote that the military life would have seemed perfect to her, '. . . if the natural modesty of our sex were not wounded by a few ugly words; I was frequently, especially during my first watches, put completely out of countenance'. So she would not stand out, Maria adjusted of necessity to the 'blasphemers and shameless talkers' and in view of the fact that, as she said herself, 'habit becomes second nature', she became quite convincing.

Maria's pious statements about her offended feminine modesty were uttered at a moment when a military court of justice was to pronounce her sentence for disguising herself as a man, and as such should be taken with a grain of salt. Maria indeed cultivated masculine traits, like pipe-smoking and fishing; in fact, she seemed to enjoy these. Her quarrelsomeness, a character trait she admitted to possessing in her autobiography, and which was later confirmed in an inquiry conducted by the sheriff of Amsterdam among her neighbours, she regretted as a characteristic of her female sex. Quarrelsomeness was indeed generally regarded as a typical feminine vice at the time.[19]

One way in which the women could betray their female identity was by not being able to perform the strenuous physical tasks required by their new professions. In the most popular Dutch ballad on the theme, quoted in the first chapter, the heroine fails in her task of binding the sails with ropes to the mast.[20] But the few documented testimonies of sea captains we found concerning their 'men' are practically always favourable. 'On voyages and watches, she behaved devoutly and honestly, as it is the duty of a sailor to be', a captain reported about his 'sailor' Adriana La Noy.

Maritgen Jans, still a young girl, had difficulties fulfilling the heavy physical duties of a soldier. She could not wield a musket, so she was given a lighter weapon. But many female soldiers must have been considered boys rather than men, and boys were usually given equipment suited to their physical strength. The unavoidable fisticuffs among soldiers and seamen also brought Marritgen into difficulties. She was, however, often defended by her loyal friend, a man named Gijsbert de Leeuw, whom she had met and with whom she had signed on in Holland. Having a regular comrade was quite common among soldiers and sailors, and it was also not unusual for the elder to stand up for the younger comrade.

The chronicler of Maritgen Jans' life provided many details about her life as a soldier in a fort of the West Indies Company on the West Coast of Africa. She was friendly and helpful, good in caring for the sick, and handy with needle and thread. For practical reasons these feminine qualities were valued in this male community. Moreover, she was thrifty and eager to learn. She could use the compass and she often took over other seamen's turn at the wheel in return for a little money. She was also clever enough to have brought a small cask of brandy from Holland, from which she would occasionally treat another sailor 'from whom he could learn something or so that he might be excused from doing that which was beyond his powers to do'. We recognise here a pattern of distinctly feminine behaviour, although the chronicler may have emphasised precisely this aspect. In the end, Maritgen was discovered to be a woman only when she became seriously ill and had to be nursed and her shirt changed.

THE END OF THE DISGUISE

Women dressed as men, time and time again encountered situations in which they risked revealing their true identities. Even so, many persisted in their cross-dressing for years. For three-quarters of the women, we know approximately how long they were able to maintain their masculine identity. One quarter of these were quickly discovered – within a few days or even hours. One quarter were able to sustain their role for between a month and six months. Half of our women lived longer than six months as men, and some of them for more than ten years, like Maria van Antwerpen (13 years in all), Catharin Rosenbrock (12 years) or Isabella Geelvinck, who was a trooper for 5 years, and thereafter a cook and a valet for ten years. Occasionally women who had been unmasked and sentenced for their cross-dressing later transformed themselves into men again. Maria van Antwerpen announced in her autobiography of 1751 that she intended to try to go into the army again, which she did eleven years later. Barbara Adriaens, who narrowly escaped a death sentence in Amsterdam in 1632, was living again as a man some years later in Groningen. Maria van Spanjen was unmasked no fewer than five times.

The majority of the women on our list were discovered; that is generally the reason why we have been able to trace them. But resumption of life as a woman could also be a voluntary act. Many of those sailing to the Cape or the Indies, for example, presumably planned to change back after the voyage. Ironically, in some cases, resuming women's clothes was precisely the reason the cross-dressing was discovered. The German traveller, Barchewitz, returned to Europe in 1722 on a home-bound VOC fleet, which also carried at least six women who had reached the East as sailors. These women apparently had not achieved their transformation back into women sufficiently unobtrusively. As a result they were sent back to Holland by the Governor-General.

However, we must not forget that discovery is a relative notion, as there were sometimes one or more close friends or relatives who knew about the woman's disguise, as in the case of Maritgen Jans. Another example is Geertruida van den Heuvel, who lived in Amersfoort for thirty years as a respected citizen of the city with a position in the city militia. Even after her death in 1838 her true sex remained unreveiled. However her relatives requested that the body be exhumed, as they could inherit from an aunt, but not from an uncle. They must therefore have known the truth.

An arrest often meant that one's person and life would be more closely scrutinised than usual, and several arrested female criminals appeared to have had a history of cross-dressing. This was the case with Isabella Geelvinck, who was found guilty of theft and arson in Utrecht in 1673. She had lived as a man for fifteen years. When, however, she found herself in difficulties because of her thefts, she donned women's clothing again. Trijn Jurriaens, a legendary fraud and imposter, was also arrested in women's attire. If the arrest was not fateful, the punishment could be, particularly when one was condemned to a whipping of the upper body. In more than one ballad concerning this subject the dénouement occurs in this way. In reality as well, this could happen. In 1747 a woman pretending to be a man was unmasked in Alkmaar on the scaffold when her clothing was removed for a lashing. She confessed that she had also been a sailor for a long time.

The risks to a woman in disguise were many and varied: lack of privacy, illness, punishment, or an inadvertently bad performance could easily mean the end of the cross-dressing. Betrayal by others was also a real risk. Accomplices could not always be trusted. Maria van der Gijsse, for example, was helped by a woman who undoubtedly received a part of Maria's earnest-money. But the latter could not keep silent, so she told her story to some soldiers in an inn, even mentioning that Maria could be recognised by a small wart on her eye. The soldiers, having become curious about the affair, immediately set out to look for Maria and thus brought about a premature end to her military career. Lena Wasmoet was betrayed as she left the recruiting officer, just after collecting her earnest-money. Her female companion cried out 'Look, there goes a woman in men's garments' after which her masquerade was of course finished. She even had a hard time staying out of the hands of angry bystanders. Quite apart from her accomplice's betrayal, Maria apparently gave an unconvincing performance, because she was drunk at the time.

The custom of having a regular comrade meant help and

comfort, but increased the risk of discovery and betrayal as well. After months of travelling and sleeping together, the comrade of Marritgen Jans, Gijsbert de Leeuw, began to suspect that his young friend 'David Jans' was in reality a girl. One day, while at sea, Gijsbert forced the truth out of her and threatened to make this known. 'David' offered Gijsbert fifteen guilders as payment for his silence. Gijsbert accepted, then attempted to blackmail 'David' into sexual contact. This she adamantly refused, even threatening suicide. After this crisis their friendship became still closer, however, and they became inseparable. Gijsbert kept 'David's' secret, protecting her when necessary, but he could not prevent her being discovered after their arrival at an African fort of the West Indies Company. 'David' became ill and was taken to the sick-bay whereupon, her chronicler writes, 'during her long illness, her shirt became dirty; for several days she procrastinated in putting on a clean shirt, because no one should see her, but in this she was not successful, because the room was so full of people and because a light burned at night. "David" rose from her bed at night three or four times, but she was too weak to stand and fell back each time. A day later, some of the soldiers came to visit their sick comrade. Entering the room, they saw that "David"'s shirt was soiled. Stating that it was not proper that he should be left in such a state, they demanded that he put on a clean shirt. Then the other shirt was pulled off and her breasts were revealed, whereupon each of them stood in amazement, to find a young girl in their company. She fell into a faint at being so discovered. . . .'

In order to avoid being discovered, the women had to be continually on the alert, especially when washing, dressing, and urinating. It often happened that a woman was discovered when she became ill or was wounded, an event which was no unlikely risk for a soldier or a sailor. Nursing and medical treatment could involve disrobing, although, as the story of Maritgen Jans shows, the standards of hygiene at the time were rather low. The 'Stout-Hearted Heroine' relates how she was wounded in the backside in battle, but was nonetheless successful in keeping her real sex hidden throughout two months of nursing. When gangrene threatened, however, the surgeon brought in another doctor to cut out the wound. 'To that end, and being completely bared by the manservants, the doctor who had been called in saw what I had till then so long hidden. "A pox to say it", he said to the other doctor, "but here is one cut more than we thought to find." The manservants, who were young wags, poked their noses in at this sound and then began to produce such peals of laughter that the house echoed with them. In short, in the wink of an eye, it spread among all the wounded that I was a woman.'

Private living space was exceptional for the common people of the time. Servants would sleep together, often in one bed, not seldom with the children of the house. Travellers often slept together in one bed while staying at an inn. The forecastle of a ship could be a most difficult place to keep one's identity secret, especially when one was sick or drunk. In the few cases where we know how sailors on ships were discovered, this usually occurred when the woman in question was not being careful enough. 'Watched by a boatswain' (Anna Jans; Johanna Pieterse); 'seen sleeping nude in her bunk by the cook's mate' (Annetje Barents); or 'detected by a sailor while pissing, drunk' ('Claus Bernsen'). These quotes reveal how four of our women were undone. Others were not able to avoid the 'ship's games' so cherished among seamen. For example, sailors passing the equator for the first time had to submit to a certain amount of tomfoolery. This was the way in which 'Joonas Dirckxe' was discovered.

There were of course other risks: a woman in disguise could always run into someone who had known her in her female past. Maria van Spanjen made the conversion into a man five times; for three of these we know how she was discovered. Twice she was discovered by old acquaintances, a third time she used the name Claes van Vliet, and was unmasked by one Hannes van Vliet. Perhaps Hannes had asked which branch of the family she had come from.

Those who were left dead or wounded on the battlefield were usually quickly visited by human vultures who removed from them anything which might be sold; and everything was marketable in pre-industrial times. Until the nineteenth century all over Europe, there were women found among the dead after many a battle. In this manner, some of the female soldiers on our list were discovered. And not only soldiers: in 1743 a sensation was caused in Amsterdam, when a stableboy who had been in service for 15 years was found to be a woman after she died.

Maybe we should be less surprised by the discoveries, than by the fact that so many women succeeded in passing as men so long under conditions of such limited privacy. People did not wash frequently nor undress lightly, but a better explanation for their success lies in the strictness of the differentiation between the genders at the time. A sailor, in trousers, smoking a pipe, with short and loose hair, would not easily be thought of as anything but a man. In several instances, children, not adults, were the discoverers of female cross-dressers, as was the case with Johanna Catharina van Cuylenburg and, the first time, for Maria van Antwerpen.[21] Modern psychological research shows that children are less easily fooled by cross-dressing than grown-ups.[22] And a story about a French female sailor clearly shows the extent to which 'men' and 'women' are culturally defined. This woman had been undetected among the crew of the explorer Bougainville for some months, but on Tahiti, she was immediately indicated as a woman by the natives. They made no automatic assumptions related to trousers and other outward accoutrements of a European male person.[23]

What the women felt after their exposure is seldom recorded. In 1765, a woman in Amsterdam committed suicide after having been discovered and taken into custody. Catharin Rosenbrock, who served for twelve years as a sailor and soldier in Holland, returned to her home town, Hamburg, when she was 42 years old. Her mother had her then imprisoned for 'bad behaviour' and also for the 'negation of her feminine sex'. Catharin then tried to take her life. Only Maria van Antwerpen, in her autobiography, shares with us her fears and misery the impending revelation of her true identity brought in its wake:

> One afternoon, while marching to the exercise grounds, the company came before the house where I had once served. As we were always strongly commanded to look to the right, one of the daughters of the house, looked me full in the face. I changed colour various times, fixing more certainly in her mind the suspicion that I must be Maria. She indicated me to her company who stood with her on the stoop, with hand and foot, interjecting that people must have been blind not to see what she meant. I thought to succumb to dismay, and fear had so seized all my limbs, that I still do not know today how I finished the weapons practice that afternoon. I could not hide the melancholy that this unexpected event lodged in my soul, so that upon my homecoming my wife could not avoid becoming aware of it, as my dejected countenance and defeated posture gave sufficient knowledge of it. There was no caress or blandishment which she

did not attempt to penetrate the reason for it, and on the pretext of sickness, which I truly felt, I took to my bed. But my inner anxiety had too much overwhelmed my brain for me to be able to taste the joys of sweet rest. Fearing to make myself more suspect, and thus strengthen the doubts concerning my person, I did not dare to remain sick for long although I never had more cause to be ill. I tried to remain hopeful that the storm would pass – but I had no chance of this. I perceived from various of our officers who were looking more sharply than was usual at me on the streets and in the weapons drill that their suspicions increased daily. Each time my service required that I must make for the captain's quarters, I found the stoop of the merchant N(ivelt) and his family occupied with a host of officers from our and other regiments, and continual bursts of laughter were directed at my passage. Finally, the terrible time came which has never gone out of my memory: it was on Ascension Day, the twentieth of May of the year 1751. The company was directed to come to the captain's quarters, to pass the newly completed uniforms. I had always attended too much to my duty to be negligent in this, although I never called there with slower steps. I was kept to the last and ordered to remain, and when I had put on the new uniform I obeyed, because I could feel in my heart where this matter was heading, and in order to lighten that heavy burden, I even yearned that the issue would be soon, as it could not be otherwise . . .[24]

What Maria is describing here is in fact nothing less than a nervous breakdown. 'Melancholy' was the eighteenth-century form of what we now call 'depression'. It seems that all the fears she had so carefully suppressed during the years she had lived as a man, came suddenly to the surface. We should not underestimate the pressure these women in men's clothing permanently experienced. Certainly, the women who wanted very strongly to go through life permanently as men were not happy as women – this emerges from many details – but it also seems likely that they were not really happy as men either.

3
Motives and Tradition

A woman who decided to don men's clothing and to follow a masculine profession for a long period of time, perhaps even for the rest of her life, made a very radical decision. The gender role change was not only very drastic but also very abrupt: the entire transformation had to be accomplished between one moment and the next. The motives for such a radical change of identity must have been weighty indeed, but, as we shall see, it is not always easy to ascertain what they were.

In many cases, the women themselves explained their motives, usually to a court of law, and in a few cases in autobiographical writings. But however interesting it is to hear what the women have to say, it is self-evident that they will have emphasised the motives which were to some degree justifiable, which were more or less socially acceptable, or which could be considered as arising from mitigating circumstances, such as entering military service out of patriotism or in order to follow a husband or lover.

But quite apart from the women's veracity, we doubt that they were themselves able to account for all the motives which impelled them to act as they did. The reasons they gave might very well have been rationalisations acceptable not only to the court and public opinion, but equally to the women themselves. We assume that for many of them, other, less outspoken, and possibly unconscious considerations played a role as well.

For a telling mixture of motives, self-justification and doubts as to whether what she did was right, we have a good example in Maria van Antwerpen, who both in her autobiography and before the court tried time and again to exculpate herself, clearly showing her own anxiety on this point. Maria van Antwerpen was a complicated case, as she also wooed and married other women, but she provides us with examples of nearly every conceivable motive.[1]

In the first place, she emphasised that God, Nature and Fate had predestined her cross-dressing. She should have been and was expected to be the seventh son of her parents, thus bringing the much-needed good fortune back to the family. 'Mother Nature has treated me too hard, against my inclinations and passions'; 'I take this as a rule, that no one can escape his predetermined fate'; 'It is impossible to control one's first passions'; 'She said she was not like any other woman and therefore it was best to dress in men's clothing'; 'She said she was in appearance a woman, but in nature a man.' Twice she explicitly stated that she was sure that God was on her side: she had asked for her plan to be blessed by heaven, and her success proved she had received this blessing. When she met a girl who had become a prostitute out of poverty, she exclaimed: 'So I could determine that without the heavenly providence of taking up arms I would have fallen into the same state.'

God's blessing was important to her. She remained a devout Catholic, not renouncing her religion when she married a Protestant. She defended herself against the charge that by marrying another woman she would break holy laws, by protesting 'that she would take (her bride) only for a sister'. Her cross-dressing, in this defence, was predestined; and then, she argued, there were others who had encouraged her: for his amusement, one master had her serve at his table dressed as a manservant; another said that she had the manners of a dragoon and looked well in men's clothing. She was forced into her second cross-dressing by Cornelia Swartsenberg, who was pregnant and needed a husband. And in addition, she was driven to it both times by sheer poverty, the first time because she had just been dismissed as a servant in the middle of winter in a strange place. As she argued at that point in her life, what other ways were open for a destitute girl? She did not want to be a prostitute, so becoming a man was the only way to stay a pure and chaste virgin. And once a man, it was natural that she marry to avoid suspicion. The second time she became a soldier, she did so to escape poverty too, as, having married a pregnant woman, she had to earn money to maintain her family.

Moreover – she continued in her own defence – others had done so and had been rewarded for it. And who could remain passive now that the country was threatened by foreign troops? She had, she said, enlisted 'out of love, affection, and a pure passion for the fatherland'. She stressed the motive of patriotism in particular to the military court in 1751.

Not all cases were as complicated at Maria's. There were different varieties of cross-dressing and a range of intentions. Temporary masquerades for carnavalesque festivities were often undertaken just for the fun of it and functioned as traditional escape from reality. During extended or dangerous journeys, it was an obvious solution to certain problems for a woman to clad herself in men's clothing. In this way they were better protected against troublesome men and were less obvious victims for thieves. For these reasons, it was to some extent considered acceptable for women to travel as men.[2] But wearing men's clothing while travelling offered women at the same time the opportunity to taste male freedom and privileges. Once having tasted that freedom, both literal and figurative, some women chose to prolong their disguise. Some may have chosen the male travelling clothes for the sake of freedom and adventures in the first place. Maria ter Meetelen, for example, travelling in Spain in men's clothing, ended by signing up there with a regiment of Frisian dragoons. The habit of dressing in men's clothing while travelling could easily lower the threshold to a more permanent cross-dressing.

The decision to start dressing as a man was never for one reason alone. The fact that female transvestism by women was a recognised phenomenon, and even had its own tradition, can be viewed as a precondition. Deeper underlying motives of a psychological and sexual nature will be treated separately in Chapter 4. First we will discuss the three kinds of personal motives that are most frequently mentioned by the women themselves: following family or lovers; defence of the fatherland; and poverty: the romantic, patriotic, and economic motives respectively.

ROMANTIC MOTIVES

The trip to the East Indies was a lengthy one, averaging six to nine months.[3] Men who signed on with the VOC knew that they would be leaving their homeland for one year at the very least, whereas many served longer terms as sailors or soldiers in the Indies themselves. People also knew that a substantial number of those who went to the Indies never returned, although contemporaries did not know the outcome of modern historical research, that this was the fate of two-thirds of them.[4] It is therefore not surprising that there were women who found it hard to be parted from their men. As a rule, the VOC did not transport women, and despite the fact that sometimes female stowaways were discovered,[5] passing as sailors still offered the best chance for women from the common people to travel to the East.

The story and person of Maria Elisabeth Meening can hardly be called romantic, but it is certain that she, in the disguise of a sailor, earned her passage to the Indies by being the mistress of the captain. This is the only case we know, and even so upside down, which resembles the situation sketched in the most popular Dutch song about the subject, quoted in the introduction. But when Maria was discovered to be a woman, the captain had to give her up, and he freed himself of the responsibility for the woman by forcing one of his crew to marry her on the spot, in a ceremony 'before the mast' which he as captain could legally perform. Maria was sent home, managed to collect the inheritance of her new husband, and when he came back from his travels abducted him with the help of her friends before he could see anybody of his family. She held him captive in her house, battered him daily and squandered the goods he had brought from the Indies.

We know several cases in which women tried to sign on to the ships with which their husbands or lovers sailed. Perhaps such couples planned to jump ship at the Cape or in the Indies and to settle as immigrants; in such cases, economic incentives also played a role. In 1667 Engeltje Dirx was taken off a VOC ship; she had signed on as a seaman on the ship on which her husband served as chief cooper. An illustration of the desire not to be parted from a husband was an incident in 1712 on the ship *Arentsduin*, in which a woman stowaway was discovered while the ship was still in harbour. She wanted to go with her husband to the East. The ship's log records the fact that the captain 'caused two sentries to stand on the poop continually, by day and by night, and until they reached the sea, against the boarding of this woman and others who might wish to conceal herself'. But the same woman succeeded in boarding nonetheless, by being taken on in men's clothing as a seaman. This time she was only discovered once the ship was at sea, but we do not know whether or not she was allowed to remain on board until the ship reached Batavia.

The story of Maeyken Blomme, who in 1611 was equally unwilling to be parted from her beloved, certainly had a sad ending. After her discovery, she was taken from the ship, and, as she promptly went mad, she was shut up in prison in Middelburg. Her transport and maintenance costs were deducted from her lover's pay.

Female sailors or marines caught on their way to the Indies often gave as their motive the wish to join their husbands and families. Anna Spiesen said that she had no family left in Holland and therefore wanted to join her father in the Indies. One female sailor detected on the war fleet in the English Channel in 1666 also gave as her motivation her desire to join her husband in the Indies. The explanation for her evident misplacement may have been the fact that in the emergency of the Dutch–English Wars she was one of those who were pressed to go from the merchant to the war fleet.

Of course, the desire for reunion with husbands and parents sounded like a reasonable and acceptable motive, being the expression of a praiseworthy sentiment in women. Sometimes the authorities even relented. Jannetje de Ridder, for example, who was discovered before her ship reached the Cape, was given permission to continue her voyage as a woman in order to reach her family in East India, 'out of which love and to which end she had clad herself in men's attire'.

It occurred more frequently in the fleet than in the army that a woman was discovered who was following her husband or lover. During peacetime, soldiers in the army could live with their wives and children. The motive of following and seeking one's love in the army, however, was popular in eighteenth-century novels and we also find it frequently in late eighteenth- and in nineteenth-century songs. In our sources, we encountered this motive only in the case of Jaantje Martens, in 1839. This serving girl from Amsterdam fell in love with a fusilier, and because her employer opposed this relationship, Jaantje ran away. She then decided to cut off her hair and dress in men's clothing to join her lover. She was provisionally taken on as a soldier in Amsterdam, but she had to report to a barracks in Utrecht. Lacking money, she attempted petty theft along the way and was arrested. Her lawyer heavily emphasised the romantic background: despite the fact that her love for the fusilier was completely run out of hand, love remains for mankind 'a source of the most noble emotions', he said.

However, not only love, but also hatred could inspire a married woman to don men's clothing. Lumke Thoole left her husband whom she had married in Emden and went to work as a manservant in Amsterdam. Another woman, who lived on the Cape in 1675, was caught 'in sailor's clothing on the beach with suit and sack and arrested . . . as having maliciously wished to leave her husband to return to her homeland with one of the returning ships'. Sometimes escape from a husband and following a lover were combined. In 1761 a lieutenant of the marines fell in love with Johanna Catharina van Cuijlenburg, a married woman. Johanna left her husband, and joined her lover, who had bought for her a man's outfit, consisting of 'a white French coat, trousers, a blue coat, another pair of trousers with gilded buttons, a sword and a white-plumed hat with a cockade'. So attired, she not only hid from her husband, but also from the authorities, who did not think lightly of adultery. But in two weeks the lovers were discovered anyway. In short, for the women whom we know to have been married, transvestism appears to have been either a means to remain with their husbands, or escape from them.

PATRIOTIC MOTIVES

Like romantic motives, enlisting as a soldier or seaman to help defend the homeland was to a certain degree a legitimate reason for a woman to dress in men's clothing. Indeed, in periods of war we usually find peaks in the numbers of women dressed as men. In the early phases of the Dutch Revolt against Spain (1568–1648) a number of women dressed as men also signed up with the army, and one of these, whom we know as Margarita, was depicted by contemporaries as a heroine. This Margarita, we read, even wrote a poem 'to rouse by her example the young daughters of the country to a love of war to protect the Fatherland'.

In the following two centuries, the Republic witnessed a number of wars at sea and at land. We often found warlike language from women who fought, dressed as men, during this period. For instance, two of the female sailors who were discovered on board ships during the First Dutch–English War before an encounter with the English fleet said that they were sorry that they had not been able to catch sight of the English. Maria van Spanjen defended her enlistment to a war ship during the Fourth Dutch–English War as having resulted from 'a great desire to serve the country as a sailor'.

The patriotic motive was certainly not always uncomplicated. The same Maria van Spanje weakened her defence considerably by enlisting more than once and thereby acquiring at least 75 guilders in earnest-money. War, or the threat of war, was of course a favourable opportunity for, a suitable inducement to, or a last push toward, the transformation into a man. The social and economic dislocation, the streams of refugees, and, of course, the great demand for sailors and soldiers often reinforced the decision to resort to cross-dressing. These women could certainly have been caught up in the excitement of war, and in their patriotism itself have seen a justification for breaking through the barrier of sex. Doubts concerning patriotism as the sole motive can, however, be found among contemporaries, such as Jacobus van de Vivere, who wrote about the women who enlisted as men during the Dutch Revolt that they did so 'for the cherished fatherland, but most especially for their own honour'.[6]

During a crisis, normal rules may be set aside. If necessary, this may include that the usual barriers between the sexes are temporarily removed or at least less strictly observed.[7] When the survival of the community demands it, women are permitted to assume masculine tasks. This may not only be observed in traditional societies but also in modern, Western countries, for instance during the First and Second World Wars. In some instances, women are not only allowed to assume male roles on the home front, but even to participate in the fighting on the battlefield. The only period in Dutch history in which women participated as women in actual fighting was during the first years of the Dutch Revolt. During the siege of Haarlem and other cities, women fought actively alongside the men. Their methods included throwing boiling tar from the city walls on to the enemy soldiers. The well-known seventeenth-century lawyer and historian, Hugo de Groot, wrote that 'as soon as God, the Fatherland, and the sovereign were at stake, a passionate hatred caused (the women) to forget more than once the propriety and duties of their sex'.[8] Kenau Simons Hasselaar, citizen of Haarlem, became a national celebrity for doing so, and a 'kenau' has become an indication for a fiery woman in the Dutch language, although over the centuries this expression has acquired the more negative connotation of an imperious, sharp-tongued woman.[9]

Apparently such a crisis situation can also help to lower the psychological threshold encountered in the decision to begin cross-dressing. Other examples of this exist in addition to the Dutch cases. In the French army, for example, during the Revolution and under Napoleon, dozens of women dressed as men and enlisted in the army.[10] The German psychologist, Ralph Pettow, who in 1922 published a book about transvestism, added a chapter to the manuscript especially devoted to the phenomenon during the First World War; among his examples, he reported a woman who posed as a lieutenant of the German hussars.[11] Thus, even in our century, war makes it relatively easy to set aside the usual norms, including those concerned with gender roles.

ECONOMIC MOTIVES

When in 1653 the Amsterdam judges asked Anna Alders why she dressed in men's clothing, she answered simply, 'out of poverty'. Indeed, a motive more important than patriotism existed in pre-industrial Europe for enlisting in the army or signing onto the fleet: sheer poverty. A medieval proverb goes that for men who had become destitute, there were always two possibilities left: they could become monks or soldiers. After the Reformation, there was little demand for monks in the Netherlands, but as Holland began its ascendance as a great sea power at about the same time, the demand for seamen increased greatly. In the seventeenth century the Dutch Republic had also become a great political power with the largest standing army, proportionate to number of inhabitants, in Europe. A man could therefore always become a sailor or a soldier and was thereby assured of at least housing and food. Women, who were already at a disadvantage because of far fewer possibilities to work and far lower wages, had no such last resort. It is true that public charity helped women more readily than it did men, but this was not meant for young, able-bodied, childless women. The typical feminine alternative of prostitution involved far less security and much more contempt from society than entering the service of the military or the fleet did for men. In fact, prostitution was as marginal as begging and vagrancy, and was defined and persecuted as a crime in the Dutch Republic.

For a great many of our women, the combination of pure necessity and the knowledge that other women had been successful as cross-dressers before, must have been the primary reason – or at least the inducement – to decide to dress in men's clothing and enter service as a soldier or sailor. The suggestion to pursue this particular means of escape from hunger and poverty also came frequently from others. Maria van der Gijsse was begging at farms, when some peasants gave her men's clothes and told her to become a soldier. Grietje Claas, a shrimps pedlar, found herself out of work when the season for shrimps was over. A chimney sweep then provided her with men's clothes.

Dressing as men also, in theory, opened up the possibility to pursue careers usually closed to women. Little use seemed to have been made of this opportunity, however. The disguised women were too poor, too isolated, and perhaps in most cases too old to be admitted to apprenticeships or schools. An exception to this was the case of Maritgen Jans. Before she was fifteen years old, she left the countryside of Zeeland to look for work in Amsterdam. At a silk-throwing workshop she earned five to six 'stuivers' a day, but that was barely sufficient for her subsistence. Before a court of justice, she later testified that she was not able to maintain herself as a woman, that she dared not return to her family, and that she had therefore sold her women's clothing and had transformed herself into 'David Jans'. She then tried to enlist as a soldier, but she was thought too young. Then she returned to her old profession, but as a man this time, and she immediately earned considerably more than she had as a girl, even achieving the position of foreman in a rather short time.

In the seventeenth and eighteenth centuries, Holland was relatively prosperous: there were no famines and the standard of living was higher than elsewhere in Europe. The Dutch North Sea coast was an economically flourishing area, to which large streams of immigrants and migratory workers made their way. Nevertheless, at the bottom of society, there was much poverty. For those who could not get by in Holland, the wealth of the Indies beckoned.

To a limited degree, ship's crew members returning from the East were permitted to bring goods back for their own trade, and use – and misuse – was made of this profitable privilege on a large scale. This may also have tempted women, or it may have been used to tempt them, as the following folk song, in which a sailor speaks to a young girl, illustrates:

He who to the Indies sails (. . .)
May there of gold and goods avail.
Be guided by me, pretty maid,
As I garb thee for a seaman's trade'.[12]

There was little permanent migration to the Dutch overseas

territories. Only at the Cape were settlements established. Nevertheless, administrators, merchants, soldiers, craftsmen, and innkeepers were necessary everywhere, and among this population, white women were a scarce and much sought-after commodity. The notion that the East was a paradise for European women developed as a result. Potential marriage partners were in abundance, in contrast to the situation in Holland, where a surplus of women existed in the lower classes. But it was commonly believed that even an unmarried woman could have a prosperous and easy life there. And there was another advantage: no one demanded an irreprehensible past. Even the lowest white woman was considerably exalted above native women. Among the female VOC sailors, certainly some must have had an eye to this easy life.

Nicolaus de Graaff, who made five trips to the East as a surgeon in the seventeenth century, and wrote several books about the Indies, is the most eloquent of those who were struck by the differences in status between women in Holland and those in the East.[13] He was particularly offended by the rich and excessive life styles of the Dutch in the Indies, and especially that of the women. He wrote: 'These females . . . are mostly so ostentatious, so haughty, so wanton, and so luxurious, that from wantonness they scarcely know how to behave. They make exhibitions of themselves; they are waited upon like princesses and some have many slaves in their service.' Dutch women, according to De Graaff, were therefore eager to go to the Indies, but this was opposed by the VOC. Women rarely received permission from the VOC to sail with their ships. If the policy had been less strict, in De Graaff's opinion, '. . . there would be more females on ships than men. Even women from the lowest spheres of life are able to marry farmers on the Cape or to set up arak cafes for seamen in Batavia, and thereby improve their station', De Graaff had a very low opinion of these women. He called them 'a pack of prison whores, drunken street pigs, and thieves, who no longer dared remain in Holland or who frequently were in peril of prison or the scaffold, and therefore had stowed away on ships or had sailed to the Indies in men's clothing'.

De Graaff considered the women who had sailed to the East disguised as men to be common criminals, not only because of the deceit they had practised, but particularly because in his eyes they had already been among the refuse of society before their cross-dressing. Or, as an English author, defending the English Mary Ann Talbot, puts it, 'It has been remarked that females who have assumed the male character have in general renounced with their sex the virtues which distinguish it, and, with the dress and manners of the other, have adopted only its vices. This censure, though in general well-founded, must not, however, be admitted without certain exceptions.'[14]

These judgements sound crude to modern ears, but we have found too many references to criminality to dismiss these opinions as mere prejudice. The relationship between transvestism and criminality certainly deserves further consideration.

CRIMINALITY

Short-term transvestism could, as we have seen, serve as a disguise which made certain forms of fraud possible, as, for example, in the cases of women who wanted only to collect earnest-money as soldiers or sailors, thereafter resuming life as women. For other women, men's clothing offered the opportunity to have a spree one evening or simply to loiter about on the streets, and they sometimes ended molesting passers-by and being arrested.[15]

We also found a far more serious form of criminal behaviour coupled with short-term transvestism: that of female members of bands of thieves who made the Netherlands unsafe during the eighteenth century. Female members of the infamous Bokkenrijders Band participated in raids dressed as men, and were no less cruel than the men. For example, around 1740, a woman dressed as a man tortured a victim during a raid by dripping hot oil from a burning lamp onto his face.[16] Such cases can still be considered temporary, but Anna Hilleghering continued to dress in men's clothing after she had joined a band in Leiden in 1724. Marytje van den Hove, who was a member of a band of violent thieves and vagrants, was a transvestite throughout her life. This relationship between transvestism and participation in a band of criminals also occurred elsewhere in Europe.[17]

Wearing men's clothing obviously was a very suitable disguise for women who embarked upon the path of criminality of their own, and we have many examples of female thieves who temporarily and incidentally dressed as men. But it often meant more than simply a disguise: in several of these cases it is striking that with the clothes these women changed their criminal behaviour from female to male. Lysbeth Jacobs de Bruyn, a 22-year-old Amsterdam vegetable vendor, for example, was in men's clothes the leader of a gang of burglars, consisting of two men and two women.[18] Anna Marie Piernau, a wife of a thief and thief herself, dressed herself as a sailor to settle an account with another woman by cutting her face with a knife; a male act of revenge. Two crossdressing thieves and prostitutes in 1714 crossed every border of female solidarity by attacking, robbing and maltreating a woman who was in a hurry to fetch a midwife.[19]

Some women occasionally dressed as men in order to commit crimes, others, like Francina Sloet and Jaantje Martens, only became thieves after their decision to dress as men for a longer period. But there were also those who donned men's clothing after having committed crimes as a woman, in order to evade the law. Elisabeth Sommuruell was to have dressed in men's clothing when she had to flee after killing a man who had tried to assault her. Stijntge Barents was accused in 1705 in Amsterdam of having poisoned both her parents. She fled, but nonetheless remained in the city, 'dressed as a sailor with an English cap on her head and a pipe in her mouth'. After some weeks she was caught and brought to trial. As she was six months pregnant, her cross-dressing had little chance of remaining undetected for long. She was sentenced, although not for murder, as no proof existed, but rather for theft and a lascivious life style. A last example is that of Janneke Jans, in 1658. She was a servant at an inn in Breda. When she was discharged, she burgled her former master's home to collect the wages she thought she was due, but stealing much more than their equivalent. She dressed in men's clothing and fled to Amsterdam, enlisting as a soldier, but she was discovered and arrested after a few days.

There were also cases of women pursuing more extended criminal careers as men, such as that of a woman unmasked in Alkmaar in 1747 when she had to bare her torso on the scaffold in order to receive a whipping. Anna Alders, who was arrested for cross-dressing in 1653, had already served a two-year sentence in the Amsterdam house of correction before. Catarijn Fiol, arrested for a series of thefts in 1691, was a member of the Amsterdam criminal scene. She said to the court that she dressed as a man to get rid of her lover. Also well documented is the story of Isabella

Geelvinck. This woman was born in Germany near the Bodensee around 1643. She left her parental home dressed in men's clothing at a very young age. After serving for five years as a trooper and ten years as a cook in the army, she left for the Netherlands and worked as a valet in Amersfoort. There she stole silver and linen from her employer, afterwards resuming her female identity as a disguise. Subsequently, she became a serving maid in Utrecht, but there as well she was caught stealing by her mistress. She was, however, permitted to fulfil her period of service. Previous to taking her final leave, she decided to strike one last blow, whereupon she set the house on fire. For this last crime, she was sentenced to death by strangulation.

Cornelia Margriete Croon forged life annuities in Groningen in 1671. After cashing them in, she made off, dressed in men's clothing. To catch her, the magistrate of Groningen had an advertisement placed in the country's largest newspaper, the *Haarlemmer Courant*, an honour she shared that year with three murderers. Her cross-dressing was not known, so she was not found. A few months later, a man, rumoured to be a woman in men's clothing, was arrested in Amsterdam for street robbery of children. After medical inspection and extensive interrogation, her identity was discovered. Cornelia was handed over to the court in Groningen, who sentenced her to death, a sentence converted to banishment for 90 years.

The criminal career of Trijn Jurriaens, born in Hamburg, Germany, reads like a picaresque novel – and it is therefore not surprising that her story became the subject of popular songs. She was an accomplished swindler and forger, sometimes working in women's, and sometimes in men's, clothing. In the latter persona and using the name of 'Hendrik Brughman', she courted another woman. She even exchanged marriage promises and slept in the same bed with this woman without her identity being discovered. Perhaps she wooed this woman to elicit money or presents, but whatever the case, after some time she wished to get rid of her fiancée. She pretended to have to return to her birthplace, and at the quay where the ships for Hamburg set sail, she took her leave of the girl. But as soon as her fiancée was out of sight, 'Hendrik' changed his clothes for women's attire, and walked back to the city.

Trijn Jurriaens' downfall was caused by her attempting a classic forgery ploy, reenacting a tale from Boccaccio's *Decamerone*. An acquaintance, an old spinster, died in 1679 after bequeathing all her money to the church. Trijn and a female accomplice hid the body, after which Trijn took the place of the deceased woman in bed. Her friend then sent for a notary. A new will was dictated in which the two women were handsomely endowed. Unfortunately for Trijn, however, this fraud was discovered, and for this and other crimes, among them her frequent cross-dressing, she was sent to prison for two years, a sentence she had to serve in men's clothing. Shortly after her release from prison she was arrested again, for infringing her banishment and stealing a wicker basket full of linen.

Women such as Trijn Jurriaens could also be found in other countries. In England Mary Frith, alias Moll Cutpurse, was a well-known figure from the beginning of the seventeenth century. Abandoning domestic service, she donned men's attire and gained great notoriety as a bully, pickpocket, fortune teller, receiver, and forger. Her life provided the material for a biography and a popular play.[20]

As many of our cases were taken from judicial archives, it can be argued that finding criminal cross-dressers is what one should expect. A criminal sub-culture clearly developed in the seventeenth and eighteenth centuries in Dutch cities, in which women played a prominent role.[21] Disguises, pseudonyms, aliases and nicknames were a regular aspect of the professional criminal culture. The use of the clothing of the opposite sex by swindlers is obviously one of the best disguises possible. However, one hardly ever finds men who dressed as women for the same purposes.

The relationship between transvestism and crime was evidently more than a distortion caused by our sources. A male disguise was not only a practical part of the repertoire of the female criminal; a more general relationship between cross-dressing and criminality also existed. Both forms of behaviour violate social rules and norms. For women who had already crossed one fundamental social boundary, that between men and women, it must have been relatively simple to set aside other norms. On the other hand, women who had already attempted criminal paths felt less intensely the social pressure which impelled individuals to behave in a way consistent with their sexes, and they must have found it relatively easy to make the decision to begin cross-dressing.

Finally, the relationship – or better said, the virtual absence of a relationship – between cross-dressing and prostitution is striking. For many lower-class women, prostitution was a last resort.[22] This characteristic they shared with cross-dressing, and it is therefore at first sight rather surprising that our disguised women seem to have had little to do with it, or did so in a few incidental cases only, such as that of Eytje Hendriksz, mentioned above, and the Leiden prostitute, Johanna van der Meer, who regularly dressed as a hussar. Dressing as a boy by a prostitute apparently happened more often, but then only as an erotic masquerade. We therefore conclude that in view of the fact that prostitutes and female cross-dressers were very much alike in age, class, and background, the choice for cross-dressing when confronted with difficult circumstances implied a clear rejection of the alternative of prostitution. Simply and generally stated, those who became prostitutes followed the female, passive, sexual path, while those who 'became men' followed the male, active and sexless path, at the same time preserving their sexual honour.

THE EUROPEAN TRADITION OF FEMALE TRANSVESTISM

The individual life histories of the women who chose to live as men reveal that, whatever the nature of their personal motives, the final stimulus often was external. In many cases, the idea was suggested by another man or woman. Anna Alders told the Amsterdam court that she had been given men's clothes by farmers, a story similar to that told by Maria van der Gijsse. To Grietje Claes, a chimney-sweep suggested that a man's life might be a way out of poverty, and he also gave her her men's clothes. A man who recruited sailors advised Margareta Reijmers to enter the service of the VOC as, he told her, 'you will make a good fortune there'. Stijntje Barents' disguise as a man when fleeing from the police was the idea of a female friend. Francina Sloet, who, after being discharged as a maidservant in Paris, had to travel back to the Netherlands by herself, was advised to dress as a man by a female innkeeper. In folk songs, too, it was often suggested by another person. The frequent occurrence of female cross-dressing in popular songs was of course in itself both a proof and a means of the perpetuation of the tradition.

The knowledge that other women had preceded them also influenced women to take this step. Maria van Antwerpen, as we have seen, explicitly mentions this in her autobiography. She may well have thought of two women who had lived in her birthplace, Breda: Elisabeth Sommuruell and Mary Read. The former lived in the city for years on a pension earned as a soldier during the war with France in 1672–78. The latter was an Englishwoman, who after a career as a sailor, and before becoming the famous female pirate, ran, in women's clothing, an inn in Breda.[23] In a small garrison town like Breda stories about these women could very well have circulated. In a work from 1766, we read that the name of Elisabeth Sommuruell 'was still remembered by many of the citizens of Breda'.[24]

Knowledge of other women who lived as men provided also a legitimation of their actions. They were aware of being links in a long chain. We can therefore speak of a tradition of female transvestism. The more or less accepted temporary forms, such as that practised during travels, festivities, and carnivals, helped to keep this tradition alive.

This tradition of female cross-dressing was not exclusively Dutch. In England there was also a considerable number of these women in the same period. And we should not forget that a remarkably large number of the women on our list were immigrants from Germany, several of them having gone to the Netherlands dressed as men. Although systematic research into the phenomenon in other countries is lacking, we presume that this tradition was mainly confined to North-West Europe. The fact that in other countries in this part of Europe female transvestism was not incidental is confirmed in the proceedings of the trial of Catharina Lincken in Halberstadt, Germany, in 1721. When she was asked what her motives had been to go through life as a man, she simply replied, that '. . . other women had done this'.[25]

While this tradition was, therefore, widespread, it remained underground. Cross-dressing never became an accepted social practice which women could choose openly. In other words: it was not institutionalised. In this, Europe distinguished itself from other, non-European traditional societies, where institutionalised possibilities did, or still do, exist for those who wish to join the ranks of the opposite sex. An excursion into anthropology may therefore be helpful for a better understanding of the European phenomenon.

ANTHROPOLOGICAL FINDINGS

Institutionalised transvestism has been found in several American, African and Asian traditional cultures. In recent years the subjects of gender roles and transvestism has become increasingly popular with anthropologists, but the interpretations they have advanced differ greatly. Also, much more is known about men who take on female roles than the reverse, which seems to occur less frequently. Research has especially been devoted to forms of ritual cross-dressing and shamanism of priests, prophets and magicians.[26]

Approaching the phenonemon of transvestism among non-Western people, anthropologists introduced the concept of liminality. Liminality denotes the boundaries and categories people make to create order in their world view. All the fundamental boundaries people draw have a deeper meaning, whether these concern the boundary between life and death, child and adult, or the natural and the supernatural. Crossing such borderlines is not self-evident and can often be dangerous. Such boundary-crossing is therefore often coupled with all sorts of rituals and vows: rites of passage. People who find themselves confronted with such a borderline, or who have a function in rituals concerned with boundary-crossing have an exceptional status within a society – as, for example, priests and doctors. Those who occupy liminal positions in one area are often attributed an intermediate position in other areas as well. Those who have a permanent status 'betwixt and between' do not engender positive reactions only, but also, and even more often, negative reactions: because they do not conform to normal social categories, they are threatening. They disturb the natural order of things and cause disorderliness, chaos and filth.[27]

Much attention has been given to an institution found among American Indians, the 'berdache'.[28] Berdache, usually men but sometimes also women, voluntarily chose the role of the other sex. This role exchange was socially accepted, but it disappeared in the nineteenth century under the influence of modern civilisation. There were never more than a handful of these persons in any tribe. In the Middle East and India, only men can take on the role of the other gender. These men, who dress as women, are often prostitutes, and toleration of them is marginal.[29]

Institutions which explicitly allow women to take up masculine roles are much harder to find. The kings of Dahomey, on the West coast of Africa, in the eighteenth and nineteenth centuries had select regiments made up of female soldiers.[30] These women, who were often recruited against their wills, were placed outside normal social family life, and they were forbidden to have sexual contacts. They were a formidable military force which was all the more feared by opponents for the dark powers attributed to them. It was considered extremely humiliating to be beaten by them. Among another African people, the Nuer, a woman who can have no children of her own may officially marry another woman. She will then have the status of a man and be the 'father' of the children her wife may have from other men. Such a woman is usually the last of her line, and in this way she is able to perpetuate the family. Moreover, her infertility is considered sufficient proof that she is not a real woman.[31]

We know only one example of accepted female gender inversion with complete cross-dressing. In the Balkans, in North Albania and the bordering Yugoslavian districts of Kosovo and Montenegro, a mountainous and isolated area, a tribal society existed well into the twentieth century. This culture was characterised by blood feuds and a strict hierarchy between men and women. Within the clans, the women had few rights and were little more than the property of their fathers or husbands. There was, however, a way to escape this state: a woman who so wished could vow to remain unmarried and to live a chaste life. As 'sworn virgins', they shared virtually the same status as men.[32] They would dress in men's clothing and even carry weapons, the most esteemed male prerogative. In a family without male heirs, a daughter still in the cradle could be declared a son by parents or grandparents, and consequently be reared as a boy. An older girl could also swear an oath to take the place of a deceased father or brother as head of the family. Here, as with the Nuer, the patrilinear origin of the institute is clear. However, this was not its only function. Taking the status of a sworn virgin was the only accepted means by which a woman could avoid an arranged marriage. According to tradition, some sworn virgins even entered into marriage with other women. The oldest documented cases date from the beginning of the nineteenth century. The theme of female cross-dressing also turns up in many, sometimes ancient, folk songs.[33] Rooted out by modern governments, this practice has disappeared, but a few sworn virgins are still alive.

Perhaps we must even search deeper to anchor the European tradition of female cross-dressing in the popular culture. In going through Stith Thompson's *Motif Index of Folk Literature*, it is striking how many variations there are to the theme of sex change and cross-dressing. Cross-dressing by men as well as women emerges regularly in fairy tales and legends from India to Ireland, and from North-America to Oceania. Men are changed into women as punishment for breaking a taboo. Cross-dressing serves as a strategem in war, or a trick to seduce women. Women don men's clothing to take the place of husbands killed in battle or to avenge their fathers. In an Indian tale, a woman disguises herself in men's clothing in order to escape an undesired lover, and in another Indian tale, a woman in men's clothing even becomes king.[34]

In Stith Thompson's work, the theme 'sex test' forms a separate category. These are tricks to determine whether one is in fact dealing with a transvestite. It is revealing that while there are only a few tricks listed to unmask men in women's clothing there are a great number to expose women in men's clothing. A few examples follow: place a spinning wheel nearby: the woman is interested, the man is not; throw a ball, a woman spreads her legs to catch it, the man does not; scatter peas on the ground: the man has a firm step, the woman falls. This last example comes from one of Grimm's tales, but we encounter it in Shakespeare's *As You Like It* as well, and this particular trick was even attributed to King Solomon.[35] In short, the notion that one must be more on the alert for disguised women than for disguised men was deeply rooted in many cultures.

Transvestism often has a ritual function among non-Western peoples and cross-dressers not only occupy an intermediate position between the genders, but also between the natural and the supernatural, as can be seen in the positions of shamans and berdaches. Marina Warner's inspired anthropological study of Joan of Arc demonstrates that in pre-industrial Europe as well, a link existed between transvestism and priestly functions.[36] Joan of Arc's insistence on wearing male clothes was related to her religious inspiration. The fact that she was seen as both witch and saint indicates that the reactions would be extremely negative as well as extremely positive.

We encountered this association with the supernatural only in a few cases. Around the middle of the eighteenth century, a fortune-teller in Amsterdam, Zwarte Griet ('Black Margaret'), stated that she had sailed as a seaman in the past.[37] Perhaps something of the sort can be seen in the case of Maria van Antwerpen, who included among her professions a period as a healer of 'evil itch', probably a type of skin-disease. It is also certain that Maria saw her cross-dressing as God-given, as her destiny; she felt that she was really a 'seventh son' – someone born under a lucky star – and she believed in omens. The case of Kenau Simons Hasselaar is also worth mentioning. She was the woman who was a leader in the defence of Haarlem in 1573. Later she was accused of witchcraft by her fellow citizens. Although no source mentions that Kenau fought in men's clothing, she is later depicted in prints as a Dutch Joan of Arc.[38] Among the non-Dutch cases, there are also only a few indications pointing in this direction. The Englishwoman Mary Frith performed as a fortune-teller, and the quack activities of Mary Hamilton may perhaps be considered as operating on the same level.[39] However, one case, that of the German Isabe Bunkens is really spectacular. In 1701, she was tried for having taken up life as a man, for twice marrying a woman, and, worst of all, for having murdered her landlady to make a magic potion, a recipe for which the head of a murdered woman was needed.[40]

SAINTS AND VIRGINS

There are more aspects which could be considered from the viewpoint of this approach. Taking on a male role and being accepted as a man is linked to the maintenance of virginity, not only in the case of the Balkan sworn virgins, but also in the European tradition of tranvestism. We have already seen how the choice to dress as a man was sometimes made as an explicit act or rejection of a dishonourable life of prostitution and as a means of maintaining virginity. It was one of the reasons Maria van Antwerpen gave, and we find another example in Anna Maria Everts, who stated that she dressed in men's clothing out of fear of being seduced by a man. Another link between virginity and cross-dressing was expressed by the German Catharina Lincken. When her judges asked her if she did not know that cross-dressing was forbidden, she answered: 'Of course she knew that God had forbidden women to wear men's clothing, but this applied to married women only, not to maidens.'[41]

The relationship between a life of cross-dressing and a life as a virgin has aspects which are more than merely practical. Virginity in many cultures is not only a physical but in particular a social quality. It indicates a phase of social transition. A virgin, in this context, is a woman who is sexually mature, but for whom sexual relations are taboo in anticipation of marriage. The state of virginity thus implies a kind of sexlessness. This idea of virginity is still very strong in Balkan society, but it was also present in Western Europe in the seventeenth and eighteenth centuries. By far the greater part of our women were unmarried, and cross-dressing served them as a means to maintain their virginal state, or in any case, to avoid having to marry.

In contemporary popular novels and plays in which female cross-dressing plays a role, much emphasis is laid on the motive of remaining a virgin. But this connection is clearest in medieval hagiographies of female saints who were able to escape a forced marriage via a miraculously acquired masculine appearance, or by disguising themselves as men. Dressing as, or even changing into, a man was a recurrent theme with female saints.[42] An early example is Saint Thecla, a woman who was so carried away by the teaching of Paul that she left her fiancé and followed the apostle. While travelling with his retinue she started to dress as a man. The transformation into a man was a very dominant theme with female saints from the fifth to the seventh centuries. Saint Margaret, for example, escaped on her wedding night in men's clothes. She became a monk under the name of Pelagius. A saint especially popular among the common people in Europe from the eleventh century on, not least in the Netherlands, was Saint Uncumber. She was a Portuguese princess who refused to be married to the heathen King of Sicily, and prayed to God to be saved from this fate. Her salvation was unusual: she suddenly grew a beard. Variations on this theme recur more often.

These female saints may all be viewed within a single pattern. They broke with their female past; they quarelled with their families; they refused to obey their parents; and they rejected their sexuality. These characteristics were not approved of in women, and cross-dressing is explicitly forbidden in the Bible. Therefore these saints pose a problem within hagiography, and the popularity of *vitae* like these has been attributed to the persistence of heathen mythology. As always, myth and reality interact, and several medieval women took these saints as their models.[43] The example that comes first to mind here is Joan of Arc. She refused to marry the man her parents had chosen for her, later dressing in men's clothing and thus keeping her status as a virgin, which was also an essential component of her charisma.[44] A later case reminiscent of this is that of Antoinette Bourignon, born in 1616, who dressed as a monk and fled her parental home to escape from an arranged marriage. She was to acquire a reputation and following as a mystic and spiritual leader, attracting even people from the elite during her stay in Amsterdam.[45]

The tradition of female cross-dressing and the connotation with virginity certainly constituted the climate in which the idea to take up a man's life was conceivable. But, of course, the personal motives and circumstances were of crucial importance. For a substantial number, there were also motives of a psycho-sexual nature. These deserve a separate treatment, which follows in the next chapter.

4
Sexuality

THE HISTORY OF SEXUALITY

The history of sexuality has attracted the interest of more and more historians in recent years, but research in this field has proven difficult with results emerging slowly. Much energy has been expended on problems of terminology – and not without reason, if we are to avoid the danger of using modern sexological terminology in an anachronistic way. This especially holds for words like 'homosexuality', 'lesbianism', and 'transsexuality', which not only have no early synonyms, but include meanings and connotations which simply did not exist at the time.

Furthermore, historians disagree on general trends in the history of sexuality. Some sketch a process of increasing prudery from the end of the Middle Ages that eventually led to an 'antisexual syndrome' in the nineteenth century.[1] Others describe a swing from repression in the seventeenth century to permissiveness in the eighteenth century and back to repression in the nineteenth century.[2]

Research into the history of sexuality has until recently concentrated on ideas and attitudes. The works of Vern Bullough serve as examples. The sources for this kind of study are mostly printed works, often by physicians or clergymen, and incidental remarks of the less-than-representative male members of the upper strata of the population.[3] But in the last ten or fifteen years, the study of the practice of sexuality and the use of archival sources have become more important. Peter Laslett and others have proven the significance for this subject of quantitative demographic research.[4] Lawrence Stone tried to reconstruct sexual practices with the help of diaries. Jean-Louis Flandrin and G. R. Quaife made use of judicial archives to study sexual life, the former for France, the latter for England.[5] All these historians concentrate on the pre-industrial period.

The study of sexual practices, especially of the common people, has proven the most difficult subject of all. Sources are scarce and often pose problems of interpretation. As yet, no generally accepted picture exists. An intriguing aspect of lower-class sexual life in seventeenth- and eighteenth-century Western Europe is the fact that men and women did not marry before their mid- to late twenties, whereas illegitimacy rates were fairly low. Does that mean that young people lived chaste lives in the ten years from puberty to marriage? Flandrin denies this, and points to the alternatives of masturbation, petting, and for men the visiting of prostitutes. Edward Shorter, on the other hand, considers it more likely that young people demonstrated very strict behaviour, at least until the second half of the eighteenth century.[6]

Our knowledge of sexual attitudes and practices of the lower classes in the Dutch Republic is very limited, but archival evidence suggests that there existed a strong repugnance among most people for any practices which diverged from the 'normal' manner of sexual contact between men and women. In the seventeenth and eighteenth centuries, freedom of choice of sexual partner, tolerance of pre-marital sexual contact among betrothed persons and outspokenness concerning sexual matters and sexual pleasures are found, but among the same people there was a genuine abhorrence of undressing, variations of sexual positions, and especially of sodomy. Prudery increased in the eighteenth century; for example, we came across horrified lower-class prostitutes who refused sexual acts like manual masturbation and fellatio, requested by upper-class clients, who would have had no difficulties persuading higher class courtesans.[7]

An important characteristic of the sexual mentality of this period was the fact that the heterosexual genital sexual act, face to face, between a married couple was the absolute standard of sexual behaviour. Furthermore, human sexuality was seen as purely phallocentric. There was, all in all, a sharp distinction between 'normal' and 'abnormal', or rather permitted and forbidden sexual behaviour, a distinction the church and the law courts also upheld. We will see that this greatly influenced the female cross-dressers and how they were treated.

Not only historians, but also biologists, physicians, psychologists and sociologists have paid much attention to the subject of sexuality in recent years. They usually make a distinction between biological sex, indicated by 'sex', and socio-cultural sex, indicated by 'gender'. One's sex is determined by physical characteristics; one's gender is determined by clothing, behaviour, speech and all

1. Print from c. 1700. Portrait of the Dutch Geertruid ter Brugge, who served as a dragoon in the Dutch army.

2. Illustration from a book of anecdotes published in Amsterdam in 1659. It depicts a woman discovered on the battlefield in 1589, found killed together with her lover. Both were soldiers in the Dutch army during the Revolt against Spain.

3. Illustration, after a portrait from 1630, of Catalina de Erauso, a Spanish 'conquistador' around 1600.

BELEEGERING
VAN
HAARLEM,
Verfiert met Vertooningen,
TREURSPEL.
Door 't Kunstgenootschap
IN LIEFDE BOVEN AL.

Te HAARLEM, Gedrukt by
IZAAK VAN HULKENROY,
a de Lange Beggyne-ftraat, in de Konings Hulk, 1739.

4. Title-page from a play (1739) about Kenau Simons Hasselaar, the sixteenth-century heroine who defended Haarlem against the Spanish enemy.

AANMERKKELYKE
HISTORIE,
OF WAARE
LEEVENS-BESCHRYVING
VAN
CLAARTJE;
Welke, in de Kleeding van een Jongeling, twaalf Jaaren lang, als Stal-Knegt, of Koetszier, in bezondere Steeden heeft gediend; dog eindelyk gelukkig aan een Ryk Heer is Gehuwd.

Den Tweeden Druk.

Amfterdam, gedrukt by de Erven de Wed:
JACOBUS VAN EGMONT.

5. Title-page from the biography of 'Claartje', a woman who worked as a stable-boy and coachman for twelve years in Amsterdam. The book was published immediately after her death and subsequent discovery in 1743. The book, however, granted her a happy end, and depicted her alive and married to a rich gentleman.

6. Title-page from the Dutch translation of *L'Héroine Mousquetaire* by Jean de Préchac (1679). This is a fictionalised biography of Christine de Meyrak, a French female soldier.

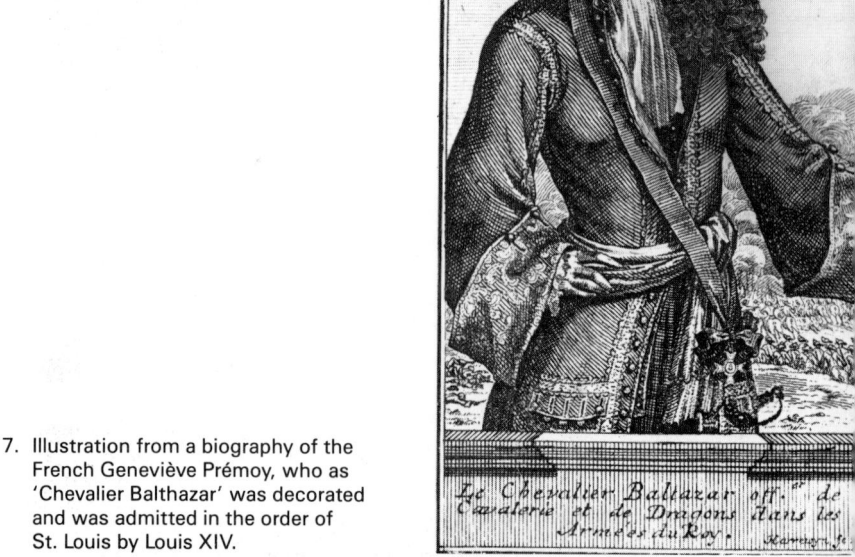

7. Illustration from a biography of the French Geneviève Prémoy, who as 'Chevalier Balthazar' was decorated and was admitted in the order of St. Louis by Louis XIV.

and 9. Anne Bonney and Mary Read, as depicted in the Dutch translation of *A General History of the Pyrates* (1725).

THE TRUE HISTORY AND ADVENTURES OF Catharine Vizzani,

A YOUNG Gentlewoman a Native of *Rome*, who for many Years paſt in the Habit of a Man; was killed for an Amour with a young Lady; and found on Diſſection, a true Virgin.

With curious Anatomical REMARKS on the Nature and Exiſtence of the HYMEN.

By GIOVANNI BIANCHI, Profeſſor of Anatomy at *Sienna*, the Surgeon who diſſected her.

With a curious FRONTISPIECE.

What odd fantaſtic Things, we Women do!
Ep. to CATO.

LONDON:
Printed for W. REEVE, Fleet-ſtreet, and C. SYMPSON, at the *Bible-warehouſe, Chancery-lane*. 1755.
(Price One Shilling.)

10. Title-page and print from the English translation of a biography (1755) of Catharine Vizzani, an Italian female cross-dresser.

11 and 12. Hannah Snell, as she performed on stage in her male guise. In this way she exploited the publicity following the discovery of her sex. Illustrations from the Dutch translation (1750) of her biography *The Female Soldier*.

THE
Gentleman's Magazine,
For JULY 1750.

Some account of HANNAH SNELL, *the Female* SOLDIER.

HANNAH SNELL, was born in *Fryer-street, Worcester*, April 1723. Her father was a *hosier* and *dyer*, and son to lieut. *Snell* who was at the taking of *Namur*, in the reign of K. *William*, and afterwards served in Q. *Anne's* wars.

When her father and mother, who by their industry brought up 3 sons and 6 daughters, died, *Hannah* set out for *London*, where she arrived on *Christmas* day, 1740, and resided some time with her sister, who had married one *Gray*, a carpenter, and lived in *Wapping*. Here she became acquainted with *James Summs*, a *Dutch* sailor, to whom she was married in 1743; but he treated her with great inhumanity, and left her when seven months with child, which dying at six months old, she decently buried it. She put on a suit of her brother-in-law's apparel, on *Nov.* 23, 1745, left her sister without communicating her design, and went to *Coventry*, where she enlisted herself in *Guise's* regiment of foot, and march'd with it to *Carlisle*. Here her serjeant, whose name was *Davis*, having

13. Portrait of Hannah Snell in *The Gentleman's Magazine*.

14. Illustrations from a ballad published in London at the end of the seventeenth century called *The Female Warrior*, relating how a woman in man's attire obtained an ensign's place.

Uytrechtse Hylickmakers, ofte Amsterdamse Kermis-koeck. 65

Een Nieuw aerdigh Liedeken van Monsr. Split-ruyter, die haer eenige Jaren, in Mans-kleedinge op sijn Frans gekleet heeft onthouden, en onder-trout is geraeckt met seker Juffrou binnen Amsterdam, en daer over aldaer in 't Tuchthuys sit, en te sien is in 't selve habijt.

Stem: Soeten Engelin.

Hoort eens wat dat 'er voor weynigh dagen
t' Amsterdam is geschiet/
Men hoeft het niet naeuw t' onderbragen/
Want ghy sult in dit Liet
Alles seer klaer na waerheyt sien beschreven
Wat dat een Vrou-mens heeft bedreven
Door het kleden als de mans/
Na de nieuwe mode op sijn Frans.

Binnen Amsterdam is sy geboren/
En haer naem is wel bekent/
Soo als een yeder wel sal hooren/
Waer men sich keert of went/
By dees en geen/ ja by 'er eygen vrienden/
Door diense haer seer mannelijck bedienden/
Soo in weesen als in dracht/
Tot een schant en smaet van haer Geslacht.
Sy heeft haer jaren langh onthouwen/
Sonder datze wiert ontdeckt/
Tot dat sy nu stond om te trouwen/
Doen de Bruydt haer bond begeckt/
Om dat 'et niet en was gelijck het hoorde/
Want sy bond 'er niets dat haer bekoorde/
Door het streelen en 't gesoen/
Daer het de Bruyt om was te doen.
Want toen de Bruyt haer gingh verstouten

15. A Dutch ballad from c. 1690, which essentially tells the story of Trijn Jurriaens.

16. Title-page of the *Kloekmoedige Land- en Zee Heldin* ('The stout-hearted heroine of the land and the sea') (1720).

17. During the first three interrogations of her trial in 1769 Maria van Antwerpen insisted that she was a man, and she signed as 'Maggiel van Handtwerpen'. At the fourth interrogation she admitted that she was a woman, and signed as Maria van Antwerpen.

18. Ann Mills, an English female sailor, from the eighteenth century.

'Mother Ross' who fought around 1700 as an English soldier on Dutch territory.

20. Illustration from a Dutch biography of the German Antoinette Berg, who fought as a soldier in the English army on Dutch territory in 1799. Afterwards, she served in the British navy in the Caribbean.

GESCHIEDENIS
VAN
RENÉE BORDEREAU,
GENOEMD LANGEVIN,

BETREKKELYK HAAR MILITAIRE LEVEN IN DE *VENDÉE*;

OPGESTELD DOOR HAAR ZELVE.

Uit het Fransch vertaald.

MET PLATEN.

Geboren te Soulaine bij Angers, in Junij 1770, met de Lelie versierd door Z. K. H. Mr. den Hertog van Berry.

Te DORDRECHT,
bij A. BLUSSÉ & ZOON.
1815.

21 and 22. Title-page and illustration from the Dutch translation of the memoirs (1815) of the French Renée Bordereau, who fought in the counter-revolutionary army during the French Revolution.

Hier draagt de Vrouw de Manne py,
En gordt den Degen op de zy,
Ja schynt den Man als uyt te dagen;
Doch Sul-oom, ang en bang voor slagen,
Verdraagt dit leet, en neemt gedult,
Wat sal hy doen? het is zyn schult.

23. Illustration from the *Narinnen-spiegel* ('Mirror of female fools'): 'Here the woman wears the man's attire/ and puts on the sword/ yes, seems to defy the man/ but that dolt, afraid of blows/ bears this suffering, and has patience/ what can he do? It is his fault.'

24, 25, 26 and 27. Details from Dutch eighteenth-century children's prints with the theme of 'The world turned upside down'.
24, 25 and 26: 'The woman goes to war'.
27: 'The girl, of weak and tender nature/ carried away with arrogance/ here we see in a soldier's uniform/ I think this is foolish'.

28. Painted canvas used by a nineteenth-century German street singer, illustrating a song about a female soldier in the American Civil War. The theme is the ancient one of a woman who dressed as a man to follow her lover into the army and dies together with him on the battlefield (compare ill. no. 2).

the other external characteristics. Genes and hormones determine the sex to which one belongs; one's upbringing and social environment are, on the other hand, decisive in determining one's gender.

Modern sexological research has paid surprisingly little attention to the subject of female cross-dressing. Still, this literature offers us, in theory, four different bases of explanation: first, biological intersexuality, second transvestism, third, homosexuality, and fourth, transsexuality.

BIOLOGICAL INTERSEXUALITY

Biological intersexuality is a matter of sex, not of gender. Many varieties of this biological divergence exist, roughly divisable into hermaphroditism and pseudohermaphroditism. Hermaphroditism, whereby a person is genetically mixed male and female, demonstrating characteristics, albeit never completely developed, of both sexes, is a very rare phenomenon. This variation is usually observable at birth and a choice must be made whether to raise the child as a boy or as a girl. In puberty, however, secondary sexual characteristics can develop and become obvious which do not suit the original determination made of the child's sex. Under the rubric 'pseudohermaphroditism' medical science has classified a number of characteristics comparable with hermaphroditism, but resulting from other causes. It refers to people who are genetically male or female but who, for example, because of a disturbance in hormone balance have (partly) the appearance of the opposite sex. A number of syndromes have been distinguished, but most of these cannot, for purely medical reasons, be applied to the women we are concerned with here. The only exception is the syndrome of androgen insensitivity, whereby in genetic males the external sexual organs are not or only partly developed. These boys are sometimes considered girls at birth and are brought up as such.

It is possible that some of our cross-dressers were in reality intersexual. However, in most cases hermaphrodites and pseudohermaphrodites who have been brought up as women feel themselves to be women, even after their bodies begin to show male characteristics. They do not desire to change their gender, and they do not spontaneously begin to feel male in their later lives. The same holds true, *mutatis mutandis*, for those intersexuals who were brought up as men. Apparently, the acquired gender identity which is established within the first two or three years of life outweighs the biological sex.

Much confusion and grief generally results when a child appears to be a boy or a girl at birth, but develops the secondary sexual characteristics of the other sex in puberty. Nowadays, surgery and hormone treatment can counter such a change of sex. In the past, it was thought necessary to reconsider the judgement made regarding the child's sex. The tragedy of being forced to change gender is evident in a number of published autobiographical works from the nineteenth and early twentieth centuries; for example, that of the Frenchman Hercule Barbin, who ended by committing suicide, and of the German who wrote under the revealing pseudonym, N. O. Body.[8]

Hermaphrodites who were brought up as women, but in later life lived as men, can be regarded as female cross-dressers. Although hermaphroditism is rare, the phenomenon was known from antiquity and it drew much attention in the seventeenth and eighteenth centuries. Much was written about it, and people with aberrant, androgynous sexual appearance were frequently mentioned as attractions at fairs.[9] The authorities also took an interest in these cases. When problems emerged after christening regarding the sex of a child or adult, they usually stepped in and had the 'true' sex determined. When this was not clear, they dictated the sex arbitrarily. This occurred elsewhere in Europe as well.

We found only one probable case of hermaphroditism in our sources. In 1675, Anne Jacobs told the magistrate of Harderwijk 'that she was more a man than a woman'. She was thereupon ordered to dress as a man. The chronicler who informs us of this history writes that she was a hermaphrodite. That information and the magistrate's decision probably mean that she was medically examined before being allowed to switch gender.

In other cases we simply do not have enough information. In one contemporary source, Marytje van den Hove, one of whose nicknames was 'Alemondus Half-man-half-woman', was called a hermaphrodite, but no details are given and the other sources are silent on this point. Anna Maria Everts had *de kwee* as a nickname. *Kwee* is an old Dutch word for a hermaphroditic cow that cannot have young; it is, in fact, the only original Dutch word with the same meaning as hermaphrodite. The German-born Lumke Thoole chose 'Schwitters' for her male surname; in itself not unusual as a surname, but a telling detail is that *Schwitter* is also the original German word for a hermaphrodite. However, this conjecture is not confirmed by other sources.

Relatively speaking, a great deal is known about Cornelis Wijngraef, a vagabond, who in 1732 was apprehended in The Hague and brought before the court. During his interrogation his remarkable past emerged. He told the court that at birth he was ascribed the female sex and christened Lijsbeth. When she was only fourteen, she was married, but her husband discovered that sexual intercourse with her was impossible. Thereupon her parents had her shut up in the 'Blauwhuis', a lunatic asylum annex prison at Schiedam. After she had been there for six months, she was medically examined by the official town surgeon at the request of the bailiff. As a result she was discharged, with the instruction to wear men's clothing ever after. Free, she – or from now on, he – left for England and there had himself christened Cornelis Wijngraef. Later, he returned to the Republic and married a woman. But his affairs apparently did not run smoothly, and it was because of beggary and vagrancy that he was arrested.

The file does not contain a sentence, so probably Cornelis was let off with a warning only. Searching for more details regarding his past, we found that Cornelis had told only half of his history. The judicial archives of Schiedam and Brielle tell other, more unpleasant details. It was true that he had been born and brought up a girl, named Elisabeth, and that as such he had married an English soldier. She – as we will call her for this period of her life – often quarrelled with her husband, and in one of their domestic fights she wounded him severely with a knife. She tried to bribe the witness of this scene into silence, but was nevertheless arrested for her violence against her husband. The court of Brielle sentenced her to ten years confinement in prison, followed by banishment. This she had to serve in Schiedam, as Brielle was too small a town to have a prison of its own.

In prison she fell in love and initiated a sexual relationship with another female prisoner. She told her beloved that she was in reality a man, and gave her a written promise of marriage, signed with her blood with the name of Carolus Wijngraef. When all this was discovered, the magistrate had her medically examined by the town surgeon, who concluded 'that she was more a man than a woman'. As a man obviously could not be confined in a women's prison, she was sent back to Brielle. The magistrate of Brielle, a small town without a prison, did not agree and ordered a new medical examination, by three qualified doctors. This learned committee concluded that the examined 'is constituted as any other female . . . no parts or members have been found contrary to this'.

On the basis of this information we cannot decide who was right, but we opt for the latter committee, which consisted of three professionals and which gave a more detailed account. The town surgeon of Schiedam, moreover, may well have been led to his conclusion by the wish of the magistrate to get rid of this troublemaker.

Pseudohermaphroditism is more common than hermaphroditism, but it is also more difficult to determine. In a still classic study, in which a few thousand cases of hermaphroditism and pseudohermaphroditism are described, Franz Ludwig Neugebauer included a Dutch woman of the seventeenth century whom he classes as a pseudohermaphrodite. This is Hendrickje Lamberts van der Schuyr, who has been cited in medical literature for centuries. She owes her international fame to Nicolaas Tulp, who gave a detailed, first-hand account of her case in his *Observationum Medicarum* of 1641. Tulp was a prominent physician and was depicted as a society doctor in Rembrandt's 'Anatomy Lesson'. He was also a member of the Amsterdam regent patriciate, holding several offices in the Amsterdam government. In 1641 he was a member of the magistrate's court directly involved in the case against the 27-year old Hendrickje, who was on trial for having had relations with other women, first as a woman and later dressed as a man. Along with this, she had served two years in the past as a soldier under the Stadhouder Frederik-Hendrik, after which she apparently had reverted to wearing women's clothes.

Neugebauer based himself upon Tulp's book, but we could go back to the more extensive original trial records which have been preserved. Hendrickje lived in Amsterdam and had a steady relationship with 42-year-old Trijntje Barents, a widow who had six children, three of whom were still living at the time. Trijntje was questioned extensively about their sexual relations, and she declared that Hendrickje 'sometimes had carnal knowledge of her two or three times a night, just as her late husband had – yes, and sometimes more arduous than he'. Trijntje also declared – possibly to make herself appear less guilty – that 'this traffic was usually the desire of Hendrickje Lamberts, who is lustful and ever eager for sex'. Trijntje told the court that she had once handed her lover the chamberpot and had seen that Hendrickje 'pissed through a shaft half as long and as wide as my small finger'. This shaft came out of her woman's parts and disappeared again as soon as she had done, so that it could be seen no more'.

This last statement suggests pseudohermaphroditism. Hendrickje could have been genetically a male who suffered from androgen insensitivity; in that case the shaft would be a not fully developed penis. However, the court questioned three other women who had been cited as Hendrickje's former lovers. All of them denied having had sex with her, despite admitting having slept with her in the same bed. All three explicitly stated that Hendrickje had 'ordinary cycles as every woman has' that is that she menstruated. Finally, the court had Hendrickje examined by three midwives, whose observations supported Trijntje's statement. In the labia near the urethra, they had found a hard part, formed like the penis of a young boy, but thicker. When touched, this 'penis' withdrew so that they could no longer observe it.

The information derived from the trial is detailed but contradictory. If Hendrickje menstruated, she cannot have been a pseudo-hermaphrodite: menstruation does not appear in cases of the androgen insensitivity syndrome. Also Hendrickje did not value her female gender identity in which she was raised, which pseudohermaphrodites usually do. At any rate, the court viewed Hendrickje as a woman, and condemned her as a 'tribade', that is to say a female sodomite, a woman who has sex with other women, which was also Tulp's conclusion.

We conclude that biological reasons will explain very few of our cases of female cross-dressing, and even then the information is hardly conclusive. No source tells of sudden biological changes, such as the growing of beards and moustaches. Moreover, the gender identity which a child acquires in infancy with very few exceptions determines the later gender identity, a serious consideration in view of the fact that we are concerned here with women who repudiated that identity.

TRANSVESTISM

'Transvestism', as used in modern psychology, has no biological origins, but is psychological in character. The term was coined in

1910 by the German sexologist Magnus Hirschfeld, and denotes an irresistible tendency to dress in the clothing of the opposite sex.[10] Transvestites are practically always men. The urge to dress as women is episodic, and at all times they remain quite conscious of their true sex. They are also usually heterosexuals. And however meticulously the manner and speech of women are mimicked and even exaggerated, it is often not difficult for the world to see through the performance.

The fact that at present transvestism is associated with men, and among women rare or lacking altogether, is a complete contrast to the situation before 1800, when men dressing as women were seldom found, whereas there did exist a tradition of cross-dressing among women. Modern male transvestism, however, is an essentially different phenomenon from female cross-dressing in the seventeenth and eighteenth centuries. The former is episodic, undertaken for a short time and meant to satisfy personal desires. We do not know if there ever existed a similar longing among women who dressed as men for very short periods of time only. Cases like Johanna van der Meer who liked to go out dressed in men's clothing, and the married Marritgen Pieters of whom we know only that she was arrested in the street in Amsterdam while wearing men's clothes, could in theory be attributed to an irrepressible urge to dress as a man, but in fact our information is totally insufficient.

We do know of cases where female cross-dressing was undertaken for the purposes of sexual arousal. There were prostitutes who received their clients while wearing men's clothing. It also appears from the literature and stories about mistresses and courtesans from the higher classes that attractive young women dressed as men. The fact that it was just possible to see through their masculine appearance was considered erotically titillating. In the theatre and in novels, male disguise by women was used to create piquant situations. But all these were meant primarily for the sexual pleasure of the men present, not necessarily for the women themselves.

Male transvestism certainly occurred far less frequently in the seventeenth and eighteenth centuries than it does today. In our sources we encountered only a few cases of male transvestism. One example is Jan Snoeck, born in Brussels, who in 1703 was arrested in female dress in the middle of the night in Amsterdam. Eight years later, he was condemned for burglary and begging in Breda.

At that time, he confessed before the court that he was 'steeped in evil, in heart and soul', and that he longed for a death sentence, desiring to be released as quickly as possible from his sufferings.[11]

To be sure, before the seventeenth century no women were permitted on the stage, so men played the female roles. After the introduction of actresses, however, men cross-dressing as a woman remained a popular element on the stage until the eighteenth century. But they were a burlesque element only, considered to be ridiculous, and not at all attractive, as the women disguised as male were. There was obviously a great difference in the perception of cross-dressing of men and women. Transvestism of men was considered much more objectionable than that of women. The man was demeaned, while the woman strove for something higher. An extremely negative opinion of men who took on a female role is also clear from the many popular prints ridiculing and censoring married couples who did not keep within the proper gender boundaries. Transvestism in men must therefore have been more strongly suppressed than in our time, when the gap between the genders has diminished. The explanation for the absence of modern female transvestism could correspondingly be found in the fact that women may dress in trousers and jackets in normal life. In short, we do not think that the modern notion of transvestism contributes much to explain why women in the seventeenth and eighteenth centuries decided to cross-dress.

HOMOSEXUALITY: THE PHALLOCENTRIC VIEW

Nowadays, female homosexuality is not a self-evident reason for changing one's sex, because women who sexually prefer women to men do not usually reject their female identity. However, in the seventeenth and eighteenth centuries dressing and living as a man made it possible to legitimise a sexual relationship with another woman. We will argue that this transvestism must not be seen as a disguise for the world, but as a step that psychologically enabled a woman to court another woman. In other words, while nowadays lesbianism is not felt as a problem of gender, in the seventeenth and eighteenth centuries it was.

The history of homosexuality is a recent, but productive, discipline which, however, concentrates on male homosexuality. In this field terminology poses real problems. The word 'homosexuality' dates from the late nineteenth century and the present content and understanding of the word is still more recent. In the Middle Ages and early modern period, the word 'sodomy' was used. In the Netherlands this word was first found in the sixteenth century. At first it was a rather broad term meant to denote sexual contact between two men, and, less often, between two women or between a human being and an animal. In practice it could even be used for every sexual act that was disapproved of. In the course of time the term was narrowed: in the eighteenth-century judicial sources it was nearly exclusively meant to denote anal copulation. Sodomy was considered a very serious sin and a crime that should be – and was – punished by death. But a great difference between this and the later notion of homosexuality is that sodomy was thought to concern incidental acts, and not one's permanent sexual nature.

In the eighteenth century a male homosexual subculture emerged in the Netherlands with fixed codes and meeting points. In 1730, during a series of spectacular trials, networks of sodomites surfaced that led to harsh persecutions. Precisely because of the discovery of these networks and subculture, the authorities no longer saw sodomy as an activity of individual sinners, but as a real danger to public order and morality, comparable to criminal gangs.[12]

In 1811, when the Netherlands were annexed to Napoleon's Empire, the introduction of the Code Pénal meant that sodomy disappeared from the books of criminal law. In the late nineteenth century, the designation 'sodomy' was replaced by 'homosexuality' and was increasingly seen as an element of one's character, a permanent aspect of the personality, rather than as an activity someone might occasionally indulge in. It was also increasingly seen more as an illness, a deviation in a physical or spiritual sense, than as a crime and a mortal sin.

The paragraphs above concern male homosexuality: of female homosexuality little is known. It had, however, a term of its own: *tribadie* ('tribady'). In Dutch this is used for the first time in 1650, in the translation of Nicolaas Tulp's book *Observationum Medicarum*. The Dutch translator simply used the Latin word from the Latin version of the book which was published nine years before. The reason is simple: no original Dutch term for homosexuality existed, neither for female nor for male homosexuality. The use of the word tribady in later texts, however, remained rare.[13]

Tribady shared the fate of 'sodomy' and was in the nineteenth century replaced by the more general term homosexuality. The history of the meaning of the terms is similar. The change from deed to character, from crime to illness, can also be seen in the history of lesbian love. The word 'lesbian', however, was introduced only in the twentieth century.

Tribady was considered just as bad and liable to criminal persecution as sodomy. However, only a very few legal proceedings are known where the sole indictment was for tribady between two women living as women. The number of cases of lesbian relationships we know of in Europe before the nineteenth century is very small indeed, and most of these concerned couples where one of the women dressed as a man. From the negligence of the courts, the general silence of the sources, and the absence of adequate terminology, much can be inferred. Until the end of the eighteenth century love affairs between women were not taken seriously, and perhaps often not even noticed at all. Presumably no one suspected two women living together of sexual relations. And in fact such relationships probably were exceptional. Most people at the time were ignorant of the existence of the phenomenon of tribady. No lesbian networks or subculture existed; tribady was far less known than sodomy; and the taboo on it was at least as great. Practically no woman did know any examples of sexual relations between women and few, at any rate of the common people, had even heard of them. Sexual desire and love was thought of as something that could only be experienced with a male. We can therefore assume that most women who fell in love with other women could not place or identify these feelings. Therefore, it is logical that those women would think: if I covet a women, I must be a man.

That in the past lesbian love was inconceivable has recently been emphasised by Judith Brown in her book *Immodest Acts*. She writes: '. . . Europeans had long found it difficult to accept that women could actually be attracted to other women. Their view of human sexuality was phallocentric . . .'.[14] Brown in this way explains the curious behaviour of an Italian nun who around 1600 seduced another nun into having sexual contact. She did so while in a state of religious ecstasy, telling her beloved that she was temporarily changed into a male angel, and speaking in a low, male voice. For both of them, this legitimised the lovemaking.

Lesbian feelings could also express themselves in other ways. Lilian Faderman described exalted, but non-sexual friendships between women from the middle and upper classes, which were quite usual since the Renaissance. In Dutch literary history there is a famous example of such a friendship, between the eighteenth-century writers Betje Wolff and Aagje Deken. Their life-long relationship was close enough to be called love, and a recent biographer classified it as lesbian, although it was certainly not expressed sexually.[15]

Lower-class women had a means of dealing with sexual feelings for another woman via the tradition of cross-dressing, whereby women took up lives as men. Once transformed into a man, one's sexual feelings for another woman fell into place. The fact that some women who fell in love with other women transformed themselves into men and even officially married the objects of their affections should therefore not be seen as an unnecessarily risky sort of deception, but rather as the logical consequence of, on the one hand, the absence of a social role for lesbians and the existence of, on the other hand, a tradition of women in men's clothing. In many of the life histories described below the confusion of gender identity caused by feelings of love for another woman is evident. A telling case is that of Cornelia Gerrits, who came to dislike her male attire so intensely that in spite of her official marriage with another woman, she changed back into a woman.

THE WOMEN WHO AS 'MEN' COURTED AND MARRIED WOMEN

Of course none of our cross-dressers formulated these ideas, but numerous details and statements point to this interpretation. Hendrickje Lamberts and Trijntje Barents began their affair as two women, but at a certain moment, Hendrickje decided to dress as a man. During her hearing, Trijntje remarked that their sexual life improved perceptibly afterwards. This must have been a psychological effect brought about by the fact that their affair then conformed more closely to an acceptable heterosexual relationship.

The logical sequence 'if I love a woman I must be a man' obviously demanded confirmation in the form of a legal marriage. We have seen how Elisabeth Wijngraaff gave her prison love a written promise of marriage. This sequence is also clearly demonstrated in the following amorous histories, both of which took place in Leiden in the seventeenth century. The first is the story of Maeyken Joosten. Maeyken Joosten had been married for thirteen years and had borne four children, two of whom were still living, when she fell in love with a young girl named Bertelmina Wale. She plied Bertelmina with love letters, which she had signed as 'Pieter Verburgh' (she herself could not write). After a short time, she told Bertelmina 'that it was not Pieter Verburgh . . . but she who had those letters written and who was in love with her'. She told her that she was in reality a man and eventually, as we read in the argumentation of the verdict, 'her vows, oaths, and sinister persuasions made Bertelmina believe this, and they were betrothed'. 'Yes', the verdict continues, 'and worse, she (. . .) had had sexual contact with Bertelmina in every manner as if she were a man.'

Despite her having a husband and children, Maeyken successfully convinced her beloved that she was really a man, extracted a promise of marriage from her and got her into bed. Maeyken left her husband, travelled to Zeeland, and returned to Leiden in men's clothing, where she told Bertelmina that the clergy could verify that she had been rechristened Abraham Joosten and that she had official permission to marry. This was of course not true, but Bertelmina believed her and the couple were married in the city hall in Leiden on 8 March 1606. What happened after this is not known, but in October Maeyken was on trial for sodomy. (The term 'tribady' was not yet used.) The death penalty was demanded, but the sentence was exile for life.

Also in 1688 two women who had been married to one another, one as the husband, the other as the wife, stood trial in Leiden. This is a clear example of a lesbian relationship that drew attention to itself unnecessarily. Cornelia Gerrits van Breugel, who had married ten years before but soon after the marriage had separated from her husband, and Elisabeth Boleyn, a spinster, had already been living together as women for a year. Then they came up with a plan which would permit them to marry officially. Cornelia instructed Elisabeth to buy men's clothing for her, to leave Leiden and go to live in Amsterdam temporarily. Cornelia followed her, dressed as a man, and as 'Cornelis Brugh' married Elisabeth in the Reformed Church of Amsterdam. They went back to Leiden as man and wife, but two and a half years later, they were discovered, because Cornelia took a dislike to men's garments and began to live as a woman again. It was the change back from man to woman that caused people to talk. They were arrested and tried, but despite the fact that the lesbian implications were clear to the court, the punishment was light: 12 years' exile and a prohibition against their living together again.

In these examples the women shared the secret, and the lovers actually had sexual relations. But this was not the rule: often the 'wife' did not know the truth. In Amsterdam in 1645, for example, an unsuspecting widow married the navvy 'Johannes Kok'. After the wedding, she discovered that 'Johannes' was a woman. 'Johannes' begged his wife to let him flee before the situation became a matter for the court and she let him go. We owe this information to the discovery of a brief notarial declaration required to invalidate the marriage, but we never found another trace of 'Johannes Kok'.

We know much more about Barbara Adriaens, whose unhappy childhood we have described above. Her family had had her incarcerated for drunkenness at the age of thirteen, and after her release she had worked as a linen seamstress and maidservant for different employers. When she was 18, she dressed in men's clothing and became a soldier. In 1632 she found herself a municipal soldier in Amsterdam, calling herself 'Willem Adriaens'. Willem's courtship and marriage can be followed in the extensive trial records.

Willem's landlady noticed at a certain point that he was interested in women and that he went to dancing places where prostitutes could be found. This gave her the idea that she might practise a little matchmaking and she introduced Willem to her younger sister, Hilletje Jans, who made her living by peddling vegetables on the street. Hilletje was eager for the match and gave Willem money, stockings, and other presents, which were meant to confirm the promises of marriage they exchanged very soon after they had been introduced. Only fourteen days after their first acquaintance, their banns were published, and a few weeks later they were married in the *Nieuwe Kerk* in Amsterdam. But Willem was soon unmasked.

Before the marriage, Willem testified later, he had shown affection to Hilletje to some degree, but had never 'indecently touched or kissed her, but only kissed her simply, as betrothed persons do'. Hilletje also kept her hands to herself. She stated that 'Willem (. . .) sometimes put his hands on her breasts or body, but without passion, and he did not persevere, because she (Hilletje) struck away the hand that touched her.' On the wedding night,

Willem told her that he wanted to have sex with her, but he had drunk too much to live up to his promises.

The consummation of the marriage continued to be postponed night after night. Willem pretended to be ill, and even alleged that he had 'the pox' – meaning syphilis. Hilletje believed this, and, she told the court, she was willing to wait for a year or two. But she was not happy. She complained to her sister, who in turn pressed Willem with reproaches concerning his neglected conjugal duties. Nor did Hilletje remain completely passive in bed. One night she began to explore her husband's body with her hands, but 'after she had felt what she did' she still doubted whether she had indeed felt anything or not, as she did not know if she had touched too high or too low'. Hilletje's knowledge of male anatomy was clearly not great. But the seed of doubt had been sown, and she finally realised the truth when a woman in her neighbourhood told Hilletje that Willem was really a woman. This woman had herself slept with Barbara when the latter still lived as a woman.

Hilletje did not dare make this discovery public, out of fear of embarrassment and other unpleasant social consequences involved. But the marriage was also not a happy one for other reasons. Willem drank heavily, and that led to domestic quarrels. One evening Hilletje came home, looked for her husband and found him drinking in an inn. In reply to Hilletje's remark that she was also thirsty, Willem answered, 'Give me nine farthings and then you may drink as well.' Hilletje thanked Willem for the honour and left the inn. Willem cried out 'For shame!', and followed Hilletje, hitting her on the back with his hat. 'You will repent that blow', Hilletje retorted and she shouted, making a great deal of noise, and revealing that Willem was a woman.

A nineteenth-century historian, Jan ter Gouw, reported without citing sources, that a disturbance then occurred during which Barbara was the victim of the *maling*, which meant that she was made sport of and roughly treated by the by-standers. Hilletje's old father then reported the deception to the city hall. This is quite possible, although we cannot confirm this from our sources. In any event, the court of Amsterdam took her crime seriously, and condemned her to 24 years' exile from the city. According to ter Gouw, Barbara's send-off from the city was also accompanied by a row in the streets.

In most cases, after a sentence of exile, the person in question disappears from sight and only by coincidence do we learn anything about his or her life thereafter. In the case of Barbara

Adriaens, we know from a court sentence which unfortunately does not give more details that she went north to Friesland and Groningen, where she again dressed in men's clothing and even married a woman for the second time.

During her trial for her first marriage, Barbara Adriaens declared that she 'regretted her deed as soon as the marriage vows were spoken'. She barely escaped a heavy sentence – perhaps even the death penalty. But within four years she did the same thing again. The urge to do so must have been very strong. In her Amsterdam trial she said that 'she had never lusted after men', and her landlady suggested that she visited prostitutes.

A last example of a woman in men's clothing who tried to marry another woman is that of Francina Gunning, whose adventurous life reflects many of the themes we have encountered in preceding chapters. During Napoleon's reign she accompanied a French captain's widow to Paris as a maidservant. On her way back to Holland she was advised by a female innkeeper to dress in men's clothing for safety reasons. On her way she was stopped by the police, and as she could not show any papers, she was judged to be a deserter, and pressed into service with the French army. She managed to escape and fled to Germany, where she voluntarily enlisted as a soldier to fight the French. Wounded in battle, she was taken to hospital and then discovered and discharged. She resumed her male attire, however, and went back to Holland, where in 1813 in Zwolle she was arrested as a thief and imprisoned for three months. Her real sex remained undiscovered. Free again, she enlisted in the Dutch army. In her lodging house, she courted the maidservant Alida Landeel, in order, she said, to get better treatment there. She promised to marry Alida. After the war, Francina did not abandon her betrothed. They went together to Apeldoorn, where a parent of Alida's lived. There they had their banns published, Francina giving her name as 'Frans Gunningh Sloet Junior, Lord of Ameromgen, 26 years old, born in Alkmaar'. This self-assumed noble birth was clearly overdone, and may have been what exposed her as a fraud: in any case, she could show no papers of identification and she was arrested. She escaped from prison, but was still thought to be a man, as appears from the description given by the police. Caught and brought before the court, the public prosecutor became suspicious and ordered a medical examination. She was sentenced to three years in prison for her deception.

As mentioned above, no form of sexual love was conceivable other than heterosexual love, no sex act other than penetration by a penis. This latter criterion made the notion of lesbian love especially difficult, and caused confusion over the definition of 'tribady' in juridical and medical writings. In his influential treatise *De delictis et poenis*, dating from 1700, Luigi Maria Sinistrati concluded that a sexual relationship between women can only be defined as tribady when one of the partners has the capacity of penetrating the other, by means of an exceptionally developed clitoris.[16] Women who are accused of tribady, he advises, should therefore be medically examined. This was already common practice: in many of our cases the first reaction of the authorities was to order a medical examination, to see if the private parts of the 'husband' or 'lover' were those of a normal female. Related to these notions was the idea that women could only make love with another woman with the aid of an artificial penis. We should probably view the imputation against Cornelia Gerrits van Breugel and Elisabeth Boleyn, that they used to have sex with a dog, as related to this idea. A similar gender confusion was noticeable among male homosexuals, although to a much more limited degree. Sodomites were often described as affecting female ways of talking and walking; in Dutch (*mietje*) as in English there exist special words for an effeminate male homosexual.[17] But even those *mietjes* did not actually dress as a woman, and never decided to change their identity completely. An exception was a man called Dirk, alias Tobias, arrested in 1767 while begging dressed in women's clothes. He was given the heavy sentence of whipping and an imprisonment of 61 years; 40 years later he was mentioned again in the archives as being unfit for release, as his 'inclinations' still were suspected. But this is the only case of a male homosexual who disguised himself as a woman for any length of time.[18] In the seventeenth and eighteenth centuries, therefore, a complete gender change constituted a solution for women, but not for men, who felt the need to express homosexual feelings.

TRANSSEXUALITY: THE STORY OF MARIA VAN ANTWERPEN

Transsexuals consider themselves to be people 'in the skin of the wrong sex'. They are the rare exceptions to the rule that one's gender identity is settled by upbringing and is fixed in early infancy. Transsexuality concerns men who consider themselves women, or women who feel themselves to be men, without any identifiable biological reason. This concept was introduced in 1949 by D. Cauldwell and popularised by Harry Benjamin in the 1960s.[19] Research into the phenomenon has produced a stream of publications, but has not resulted in an acceptable, definitive explanation of the causes. As the publicity surrounding transsexuality has escalated, so has the number of people who apply for sex-change operations. Although until recently the vast majority of known transsexuals were male-to-female, the female-to-males are catching up in numbers, and recent figures and theories suggest that there may now be as many female-to-male as male-to-female transsexuals. It is possible that some of our women were transsexuals. In only one case, however, do we have rather clear indications of it: Maria van Antwerpen.

We have introduced Maria while discussing other topics above, but we will outline here the complete story of her unusual and fascinating life. She was born in Breda in 1719, became an orphan in her early teens, and was brought up chiefly by an aunt who treated her badly. Her life is well-documented until 1769. Curiously enough, we know nothing of the years between 1732 and 1740, and it is remarkable how cleverly she evaded this period in her autobiography and during questioning at her trial. This suggests that she had experiences she did not wish to be reminded of or did not wish to see raked up.

In 1740 she lived in Breda, working as a maidservant. She changed employers a number of times, in itself not unusual, and in 1746, when she was 27 years old, she left with the family she was serving at the time for Wageningen. There she was dismissed because she had stayed away longer on a Christmas visit to her family in Breda than had been agreed. In mid-winter in Wageningen, which is situated in a poor, rural area in the East of the country, there was no work available. She had no friends or relatives there. Something had to be done.

Maria was afraid of being compelled to become a prostitute, and she had heard of women who had gone into the army: those were the reasons she gave for her decision to don men's clothing and become a soldier. After her change of dress she left Wageningen in the middle of the night and was approached the next day on a country road by a recruiter for the army. She let herself be led away to a pub and, once drunk, signed a contract as 'Jan van Ant, 16 years old'. In this manner she embarked upon a wandering life. Her unit was constantly on the march and encamped in different locations, in part because of the war against France. By chance, Maria never did active service in a battle, a fact which she regretted.

'Jan van Ant' quickly adapted to the soldiers' life, although the fear of discovery never left her. As soldiers have always had a reputation as lovers of women, Maria said in her autobiography that Jan too courted servant girls and widows to remove all suspicions – and quite successfully too. Moreover, courting a servant girl often meant scraps from her master's table and even presents out of her savings for the badly paid soldiers. When Jan's unit was encamped in Coevorden, he met the daughter of a sergeant, Johanna Kramers, with whom the flirtation quickly became serious. They were officially married in August 1748. The bride did not know that her husband was a woman, so Maria took a great risk. But there were real advantages too, which could rationalise the step. A common soldier had no privacy, but a soldier who married could set up his own household and was thus liberated from communal life. In a pre-industrial society, married existence gave more economic security and comfort than bachelorhood, provided the marriage was not encumbered with too many children, a risk Jan could well afford to take. After his marriage Jan began to work as a tailor in his considerable free time, whereas his wife took in washing and looked after foster children. Financially they did very well. To the outside world, Jan's role as a man was complete. A practising soldier, a tailor, a (foster) father, who is described as a pipe-smoking patriarch, fond of fishing.

Nonetheless, Maria created more problems than she solved. At night the man's role was harder to perform. Jan succeeded in avoiding sexual contact by continually feigning moodiness and illness. Her wife resigned herself to this, but it made her unhappy and she was saddened by her childlessness. In three years of marriage, she never discovered Jan's true sex.

Jan's discovery in Breda in 1751 by a member of the family she had served was a heavy blow for Jan and Johanna. Maria's ordeal we have encountered before, but Johanna's shock and humiliation must have been worse. She was shouted at and joked at in the streets, and in all probability, after Maria's trial and banishment they never met again.

After her discovery, exiled from Breda and other garrison towns, Maria wandered around for a time in women's clothing, but within a year she went to live in Gouda, where one of her brothers worked. She earned her living by sewing. There she befriended a young girl named Jansje van Ooijen, the niece of her landlady. They went to live together in Rotterdam while Maria earned a living as a seamstress. After three and a half years, Maria brought Jansje back to her aunt, because, in her own words, she had too little work to be able to maintain her. This statement, and other details, suggests the role of a husband. Did she have a love affair with her protégée? That was also what the court wanted to know, and in answer to the question 'whether she had debauched or seduced the said Jansje van Ooijen', Maria replied, somewhat mysteriously, that it 'had been with the consent of Jansje van Ooijen's aunt'. The court did not press their questions on this point further.

The year 1761 found Maria again living in Gouda, still in woman's clothing, but occasionally dressed as an 'amazon', which probably meant that she wore trousers, but was nonetheless recognisable as a woman. In this period, she met Cornelia Swartsenberg. Maria made the first advances and the infatuation came from her side as well. Cornelia, who apparently knew of Maria's past, needed a man because she was pregnant. She persuaded Maria to live as a man again and to marry her. This time, Maria chose the name 'Machiel van Handtwerpen'.

In 1762, the two women entered into wedlock officially in Zwolle, where another member of Maria's family lived. The child that had been the immediate stimulus for the marriage was born dead, but Cornelia became pregnant twice more. One pregnancy ended in a stillbirth, but the second in the birth of a boy who was baptised Willibrord van Hantwerpen. One of Maria's brothers and his wife were present as godparents at the baptismal ceremony. For some time Maria maintained to the court that she had begotten these children herself, even after she had admitted to being a woman. Thereafter, she said that Cornelia, who was a washerwoman, had been raped when she was delivering washing. The judges, however, suggested instead that Cornelia was a prostitute and that Maria had shared in the profits of her trade. Maria denied this, and there are no further indications supporting this notion. It seems much more probable that Cornelia lived a profligate life and in fact took advantage of Maria.

After her second transformation, Maria went into service as a soldier in Zwolle. Maria said that Cornelia urged her to do so in order to ensure that there was bread on the table. After only a few months, she left the army again because of a conflict over her period of service. The couple left for Amsterdam. There Maria – or rather Machiel – earned a living by making clothing, selling orange ribbons to Orangists, dealing in second-hand goods, and curing skin diseases. In 1764, Maria entered service as a soldier for the third time, as a municipal soldier in Amsterdam, but at the end of 1768, she was discharged because of her 'quarrelsome nature'.

Shortly after her dismissal she went with Cornelia to Gouda to visit old acquaintances. There she was recognised by someone at an inn. It was Cornelia, however, who made such a disturbance that the bailiff was summoned. Cornelia succeeded in eluding the hand of justice. She went back to Amsterdam and then disappeared, while Maria bore the brunt of the consequences, even protecting her friend by lying about Cornelia's possible whereabouts. After an extended trial during which the bailiff had inquiries made in other cities, Maria was sentenced a second time to exile. We know little about the lives of the women after this. Maria was turned out of Gouda; Cornelia returned there to live, but later left for Turnhout in the Southern Netherlands. Finally, we know that Maria died in her birthplace, Breda, in 1781 and was buried in a pauper's grave.

Both times Maria took up a life as a man, she did so for reasons that are already familiar: the threat of impending poverty and the awareness that other women had done so – the second time her own experience. In her case other factors are clearly visible. There is one indication of a biological explanation for Maria's crossdressing, coming from the description of a remarkable experience she had during puberty. When she was about seventeen years old, she told the court, she noticed that 'something like a shaft shot out of her body whenever nature demanded the discharge of seed'. This could have been an indication of (pseudo)hermaphroditism, certainly in combination with the fact that she had a rather male appearance. But Maria was twice medically examined, in 1751 and 1769, and both times the conclusion was that she was anatomically female. There are no other indications of intersexuality.

In her case, transsexuality is arguable. Maria certainly preferred women to men, but her first decision to dress as a man was not caused by love for another woman. Maria always denied having had sexual contact with either of her spouses, instead stating that they had always lived 'like sisters together'. This was of course true for her first marriage, and although it can have been said out of fear of a conviction for tribady, it could equally have been true for her second marriage. Modern sexological theory holds that some transsexuals are oriented toward external acceptance as a member of the opposite sex only, and in such cases, sexuality plays no role or only a limited one. Maria's relation with Jansje van Ooijen may have been less platonic, however, although the wording here is not clear.

Transsexuality is definitively suggested by several statements made by her during her trial in 1769. At a certain point in the interrogation, the magistrates, confused by Maria's answers and appearance, asked her if she was a man or a woman. Maria answered, 'By nature and character, a man, but in appearance, a woman.' In her autobiography, we find this expressed in a more literary manner: 'It often made me wrathful that Mother Nature treated me with so little compassion against my inclinations and the passions of my heart.'[20] These remarks may be compared to that often heard from transsexuals, that they feel 'trapped in the body of the wrong sex'.

Another declaration she made at her trial in 1769, that even during the time when she dressed as a woman, she 'always wore men's dress underneath', confirms this. Wearing men's underwear must have been for her an expression of her belief that she was really a man. This occurs more often among transsexuals nowadays, when a complete change of gender is not yet undertaken. Also the statement concerning the 'shaft' which shot outward can indicate transsexuality. The psychologist Robert Stoller observed the irrational conviction of having a penis among modern transsexual women.[21] Maria's insistence, for some time after she admitted to being a woman, of having fathered the children of Cornelia, is to be seen in the same light.

It is furthermore remarkable how completely at home Maria felt in her role as a man. She was so convincing that the magistrates of

Gouda continued to refer to her as 'him' and 'Machiel' until the fourth hearing. During her second marriage, her 'fatherhood' made such an impression on Maria that five years later she was still able to tell the magistrates precisely how long the little Willibrord lived, to the day and to the hour. As a maidservant, she spent her savings on a silver snuff-box, a rather male item to which she was much attached.

Transsexuality is a much discussed problem, for which neither cause nor cure has been found. Some writers even suggest that it recently has been 'invented', which would mean that the term cannot be applied to earlier times. Lothstein, a psychiatrist who has treated many female-to-male transsexuals, judges it to be a severe disorder caused by a distorted upbringing that failed to give the girl in question a stable gender identity. His case studies show extremely unhappy family lives. Moreover, he states that many transsexuals do not really feel themselves to be men, but are lesbians who dare not admit this to themselves out of abhorrence of 'unnatural' sexuality.

In our opinion, Maria van Antwerpen certainly makes a case for the existence of transsexuality before the introduction of the word by modern science. At least 17 of the 21 points of a much-used checklist drafted by Sorensen and Hertoft to diagnose female-to-male transsexuality, readily apply to her. It is possible that this conclusion may also be drawn for some of the other women we studied; however, only in this case do we have sufficient information to establish a certain degree of probability.

FROM TRIBADES TO LESBIANS: A THEORY

Rather unexpectedly, the study of female cross-dressing in early modern Europe gave us new ideas and insights in the history of female homosexuality. Starting from our findings on the seventeenth and eighteenth century, we argue that lesbian love has for the last four centuries passed roughly through three stages. Until the end of the eighteenth century the existence of sexual feelings of women for other women was nearly inconceivable. Sex was seen as an exclusively heterosexual act, for which the penis was indispensable. Women who fell in love with other women therefore often doubted their gender, and the tradition of female cross-dressing offered them the solution of 'changing into a man', a choice which also brought other social and financial advantages.

For male homosexuals, the situation was different. As both men possessed a penis and love for a man was, given the hierarchy of the sexes, more logical than love for a woman, sexual relationships between men were far better conceivable than between women. Still, among male homosexuals in the seventeenth and eighteenth centuries gender confusion was not uncommon, either. But for men, to change sex completely meant a great social and psychological degradation. In spite of frequent effeminate behaviour and female nicknames, homosexual men did not pass as women for any length of time.

Around 1800 the situation seemed to be changing. The sensation and publicity that surrounded the persecutions of male sodomites from 1730 onwards undermined the notion of sex as only possible between a man and a woman. Napoleon's law reforms made sodomy disappear from the books of criminal law, and on the continent no homosexual faced the death penalty anymore. It was at the end of the eighteenth century, in 1792, that in the Netherlands lesbian relationships came to the surface where none of the concerned dressed as a man. In that year, Elisabeth Wiebes and Bartha Schuurman were arrested in Amsterdam and charged with having murdered another woman. Elisabeth and Bartha were lovers, but when the former befriended another woman, Bartha, in a fit of jealousy, killed her rival with a knife. This sensational case was followed by some ten other arrests of women in Amsterdam in the next six years, who were accused of 'dirty caresses of one another'. The accused were all very poor, marginal women.[22] We have no proof that such lovemaking between women as women did not occur earlier, but they are the first to be mentioned in Dutch sources, whereas to our knowledge Francina Gunningh Sloet, in the beginning of the nineteenth century, was the last Dutch cross-dressing woman who courted other women.

In other countries examples of lesbians who passed as men in all respects were also becoming very rare in the nineteenth century. In this era sexology as a science developed, ideas on sexual behaviour became less fixed, and sexological knowledge spread. Only in the second half of the nineteenth century, however, did female homosexuality begin to attract scientific attention. The idea that two women could have a sexual relationship became gradually more conceivable. But it was still impossible to see and describe lesbian relations other than in terms of the married couple, with heterosexuality and strict gender division firmly established.

In 1869 the German psychiatrist Carl von Westphal published an influential case study about what he called a 'congenital invert', a young woman who from childhood on preferred to dress as a boy, and had always been attracted to women. This woman behaved like a man, but she did not completely change her identity. Westphal's description and diagnosis was the first of a whole series of articles in medical journals on the phenonemon of a woman who loved women. Such a one was declared to be a pervert, an 'homme manqué', even when she dressed and lived as a woman, as was now usually the case. She who was the willing subject of these attentions was considered a normal woman.

This image of lesbian couples, one an unnatural human being, the other her victim, was popularised in the writings of the time. On the one hand a lesbian couple was judged a 'perversity', but on the other hand the 'butch-femme' pattern described agreed very well with the social norms, as it perfectly mirrored the accepted idea of what a married couple should be. This 'butch-femme' type of female homosexual relationships was only partly an invention of the medical science of the time. In the nineteenth century, these descriptions, however ideologically coloured, were probably in accordance with reality. Like the sexologists, the lesbians of the nineteenth century must have found it easier to conceptualise love between women in terms of the dominant ideas on sexuality and marriage. Again we can make here a comparison with male homosexual couples of the time, where it was also common that one partner took on the male role, and the other the female role.[23]

Only in the 1960s did homosexuals free themselves from the model of the traditional, gender-divided couple. The right was claimed to give love between two women or two men a place and a style of its own. Among young lesbians, the butch-femme type of relationship fell into discredit, and masculine behaviour was rejected as being still influenced by the heterosexual norm. Of course, this development had its counterpart in heterosexual relations, which have shed much of the rigidity of gender role divisions during the same period.

Within current lesbian subcultures, it is emphasised that homosexuality does not mean a rejection of one's gender identity.

This means that lesbian women have now arrived at a position that is the very opposite of the cross-dressing tribades of two and three centuries ago. The former cultivate a gender identity that is emphatically female, maybe more so than heterosexual women, while the latter conformed to the male gender role, and, to judge from the frequent stories of heavy drinking, swearing, and fighting, even exaggerated their masculine behaviour.

5
Condemnation and Praise

In the eighteenth century, many Dutch cities had anatomy theatres, with collections of misformed babies preserved in alcohol, stuffed animals and human skeletons. The theatre in Rotterdam acquired a rather grotesque attraction around the middle of this century: the prepared and stuffed skin of a woman called Aal the Dragoon. This was placed, sword in hand, upon the carcass of a horse. Aal had served as a dragoon for many years when she was stabbed by a fellow soldier in a fight over a game of cards. The fact that her body was subsequently put at the disposal of medical science and that her remains were thereafter to serve the purposes of instruction must be considered posthumous punishment, because only the most serious cases among criminals were denied burial at the time.

The posthumous treatment given another female soldier about a century earlier whose sex was also discovered only after her death stands in stark contrast to that given Aal. Trijntje Simons, alias 'Simon Poort', was buried in the garrison town Rees with military honours, and military and naval commanders, as well as the local municipal authorities, were present at the ceremony. Her father took it upon himself, moreover, to have a memorial stone placed on her grave, because he felt that 'such brave deeds by a woman should not be forgotten, but are worthy of being lodged in the hearts and minds of the Dutch people'.

In this chapter, we will examine the contemporary reactions to female cross-dressing, of the authorities, of those in the women's environment, and of public opinion in general. The stories above show that the treatment given female cross-dressers could differ greatly, and more such contrasting examples could be given here. To cite but one, several women who were discovered on board VOC ships were condemned as criminals, but Francijntje van Lint was permitted to disembark at the Cape and to seek a husband there, because authorities viewed her case as 'an evident example of God's wonderful direction in all things'.

At first glance this diversity in reactions appears arbitrary, but closer study shows clear patterns, which, however, do leave some reactions unexplained. First, the position of those who reacted to these women made a difference. Judges must adjudicate cases: they may punish or set free those brought before them, but they can never reward. At most, they may close their eyes to a phenomenon such as cross-dressing. Therefore, in our most important sources, we can hardly expect to find positive reactions. On the other hand, the officers and captains who were confronted with disguised women could not ignore cross-dressing, but were instead obliged to take action in all cases. A female soldier or sailor was a considerable source of annoyance to them, but she was also a possible means of propaganda. Officers were free to commend individuals and reward services rendered, but they had little power to punish the women themselves beyond the unavoidable dismissal.

A pattern that can be discerned is the difference in reactions between the common people and the elite. Negative feelings predominated among the lower classes, whereas the elite showed more nous, comparing the women to legendary heroines, and citing other, often literary examples. But this sophistication is seen most often when stories and second-hand experiences of transvestism were concerned. Those who discovered a case of cross-dressing in their midst were deceived at that point where one normally encounters the first and most important criterion in relationships with others: the knowledge that one is dealing with a man or a woman. Unexpected direct confrontation with a woman in disguise very often provoked negative emotions.

But the most important variation in reactions to these women was dependent upon the nature of the motives and degree of success of the disguised woman, as well as the degree to which she was guilty of other offences. It was judged that a woman who became a man strove to become something better, higher, than she had been, and that was considered an understandable and commendable effort in itself. If she was successful, one had to admire her. Scorn and rejection, however, were her part if she failed. If the cross-dressing was instigated by patriotism or family feelings – praiseworthy sentiments in women – then she might be judged mildly. If, however, the fraud of disguise was used for further deception and criminal practices, the reaction was extremely negative. Considered the worst of these practices was the perversion of a relationship or even marriage with another woman:

not only the natural order of things, but also religious consecration of the divine order was mocked.

Practically all reactions discussed above are male. It is, however, likely that among the hostile by-standers and singers of jeering songs there were also women. Within the women's culture cross-dressing may have been thought of and talked about in a different way, but of that we have no information. We found only one written testimony by a woman, and her reaction is very suggestive. On 11 May 1769 a young girl wrote in her diary: '(Today) . . . I had with much emotion ample food for thought. It was about a prisoner I saw being driven along: a woman in men's clothes who was fetched from a barge by the sheriff of Rotterdam; she was deadly pale and the sight disturbed me deeply. I sat brooding on it all evening . . . '.

LEGISLATION AND THE BIBLE

Dutch law drew from many sources: common law, Roman law, Canon law, and, very important in the Calvinist Netherlands, the Bible. The Bible contains a clear prohibition regarding cross-dressing: 'The woman shall not wear that which pertaineth unto a man, neither shall a man put on a woman's garment: for all that do so are abomination unto the Lord thy God' (Deut. 22:5). This Biblical text was sufficient to make cross-dressing a criminal offence, even if the act was not included in contemporary compilations of criminal law. It was persecuted and brought before courts, but many of the trials we know of were of women who had also committed another offence. The reason for this could be, of course, that women who were guilty of dressing as a man only were generally left in peace.

Legislation and the administration of justice were extremely decentralised in the Netherlands.[1] Most of our cases were dealt with by municipal courts: a minority came before provincial courts or military courts. Because the bureaucracy was somewhat careless in the period and not all archives have been preserved, it was not always possible to recover information concerning the procedures followed and verdicts reached. Other sources such as newspapers sometimes provided supplementary information.

In a fragmented judicial system such as that of the Dutch Republic, problems of jurisdiction easily arose. Female soldiers could pose a problem of juridical competence, as is shown in the case of Maria van der Gijsse. Maria was a soldier, but she fled from the army when she learned that the woman who had helped her had betrayed her and discovery was imminent. She was arrested in the countryside as a deserter by an ensign. The ensign turned her over to the bailiff of the village of Brummen in Gelderland. But a juridical question arose: did Maria fall under the legal administration of the military as a deserter or the civil administration as a woman? An elaborate correspondence followed, moving upwards in hierarchy till it reached the Provincial Court of Law, which in the end decided to take over the responsibility for the case itself.

JUDICIAL AUTHORITIES

As no punishment for cross-dressing was prescribed in Dutch legal literature, and courts had to deal with the phenomenon infrequently, no consistent procedures were established. It is also difficult to distil the penal practice from the sentences, as we know of few cases of trials for cross-dressing only.

Temporary transvestism during festivities was an old folk custom and was therefore tolerated, unless the festivities got out of hand. The Amsterdam woman who had joined a bridal feast in cross-dressing in 1784 was sentenced to a fine of 100 guilders and six weeks in the workhouse. But this procession had turned into a political demonstration, and this was the true focus of attention during her trial.[2] In the same city, a serving maid came before the court in 1701 for having dressed in men's clothing, and, together with the son of the house where she was employed, having visited a brothel and participated in other revelry. This of course aggravated the offence, but she was let off with a reprimand nonetheless.[3] A more severe punishment had been prescribed under similar circumstances in 1783. The woman declared before the court that she did not realise that there was any harm in their actions, but she and her friend were each fined 100 guilders. It is likely that their drunkenness and rowdiness on the street were also taken into account.[4]

We already pointed out that women who had crossed the threshold between genders apparently found other forms of deception easier to undertake as well. For a number of women, the offence in question concerned the collection of earnest-money as soldiers or sailors and their subsequent failure to turn up for induction or embarkation. This form of fraud was often practised by men, who when caught were punished with the forfeiture of several months pay, and, of course, they had to fulfil their service. For this offence women were punished with a reprimand or exile. The sentence for women who inadvertently betrayed themselves soon after actually entering service varied from some weeks to a year in a workhouse or prison, or they were condemned to exile, the pillory, or whipping. The punishment was also related to attendant circumstances. This may be seen in the case of Maria van Spanjen, who enlisted five times around 1782, four of which were for service with the war fleet. After the first time, when she was able to maintain her disguise for eight months, she was not punished. The second time, when she was quickly discovered, she was shut up for a week and a half in the Rotterdam Admiralty Court: her failure as well as her relapse led to an; albeit light; sentence. No sentence is known for the third and fourth attempts. The fifth time, she also committed a theft and collected earnest-money more than once, so she was sentenced to a year in prison. The crimes against property she had committed, together with her repeated relapses, contributed to the severity of the sentence.

Women who used cross-dressing to embark upon a path of crime received sentences which were in the first instance determined by their crimes, but the judges viewed their masquerade as an indication of the depravity of such women. The aspect of disguise certainly played a role in influencing the court, as is clear from the verdict pronounced over the swindler Trijn Jurriaens. She was exposed on the pillory and had to serve her prison sentence in men's clothing, making her an object of interest and ridicule in the Amsterdam prison, which was open to the public as a tourist attraction. Lumke Thoole represented a similar case. She was unmasked en route to the Cape, but she was permitted to settle there as a woman. She married, but a few years later she was recognized by her first husband who as a sailor coincidentally landed at the Cape. Lumke Thoole was sentenced to the pillory for bigamy, exiled to Europe, and fined 100 *rijksdaalders*. It is clearly stated in this sentence that her cross-dressing of two years before was taken into consideration in the punishment prescribed.

Women who had a relationship with or who had even married other women while in men's clothing comprised a very different group. They were suspected of sodomy or tribady, which was definitely established as a capital offence. Most legal texts concerned themselves with male homosexuality, but texts also existed which dealt with sexual contact between women, such as Roman law, which prescribed beheading, and the Constitutio Criminalis of Charles V, which prescribed death by fire. These were important legal sources during the Dutch Republic. The judgement of the French jurist, Jean Papon, who recommended the death penalty for lesbian women in the beginning of the seventeenth century, was also cited in the Netherlands.[5] The fear of Maria van Antwerpen, expressed in her autobiography, that she might be put to death, was certainly justified in terms of legislation.

In spite of the prescribed death penalty for tribady, amorous relationships between women, even when these were coupled with physical caresses, were rarely viewed as serious throughout Europe. Notions concerning sexuality were so phallic–genital oriented that two embracing women were viewed as relatively innocent. In sharp contrast to the fate of male homosexuals, only a few trials of a lesbian sexual relationship as a single crime have been found in Europe, and even fewer executions. In the Netherlands, no lesbian relationship as a sole offence has been found to have been tried by a court until the very end of our period. Between 1796 and 1798 several women were sentenced in Amsterdam to a few years in prison, thus receiving very much lighter punishments than male sodomites.

Until the end of the eighteenth century, only in cases in which one of a female couple dressed as a man, and particularly when official marriages were involved, were accusations of sodomy sometimes made. But even in such cases no one knew quite what to do about it. The second trial of Maria van Antwerpen, when she admitted to having 'seduced and debauched' a girl she had been living with, provides a remarkable example of this. The court simply passed over the significance implicit in this statement, and did not ask further questions.

Homosexual relationships between two women living as women were therefore in fact not punished and were even ignored, in glaring contrast to the death penalty which was applied without the possibility of pardon to male homosexuals. When sexual relationships between women were concerned, the courts were very hesitant to draw the conclusion that sodomy was involved and even more reluctant to prescribe its attendant punishment. In some cases we know that the death sentence was debated among the judges, as in the case of Hendrickje Lamberts van der Schuyr in Amsterdam in 1641. The court considered Hendrikje's offence very serious, as she 'not only dressed in men's clothing despite the fact that she is a female person in all parts, but also – and much worse – she had entered into a relationship with one Trijntje Barents . . . against all natural order, as if the one had been a man and the other a woman'. The sentence, however, was whipping and twenty-five years exile from the city. Trijntje Barents was also sentenced to be whipped but she was not exiled. She was in fact kept in the city precisely because the intention was to keep the two women apart.

In many of these cases, the women who dressed as men married their betrothed officially. This mockery of the religious ceremony was naturally considered to be a serious offence. The one who took on the man's role was always considered to be the guilty party. In reality this was not always so, but it did frequently happen that the 'woman' did not know that her lover, bridegroom or husband was not a man. This, of course, aggravated the deception. The motivation behind the verdict pronounced by the military court concerning Maria van Antwerpen, who as 'Jan van Ant', had married Johanna Kramers, was expressed as follows: 'because the prisoner has deceived and misled the whole world and especially the previously stated Johanna Kramers in a scandalous and abominable manner by such an extreme and unnatural change and counterfeit of name and quality, and beyond this had defrauded and deluded the institutions and edicts of the land, which in a nation of justice may not be countenanced but must rather be punished so as to make an example of it'.

Her punishment was exile from the districts of Brabant and Limburg, and – possibly to avoid the risk of a relapse – from all garrison cities. Of her second trial we know the sentence demanded for this offence, as well as the verdict reached. The prosecutor called for whipping, branding, twelve years in the house of correction and banishment for life from all of Holland, but the magistrates finally considered life-long banishment from the city of Gouda sufficient. In the final indictment tribady was not mentioned.

Maeyken Joosten, who left her husband and children for a woman, whom she later married, was directly accused of sodomy. The prosecutor stated that her deeds and those of her lover were 'matters of most evil consequence, bringing down the anger of God upon cities and countries and reeking of the inexcusable sin of sodomy, which according to God's law and all civil edicts, is forbidden upon pain of severe punishment and penal law'. The punishment he called for, therefore, was that the prisoner 'shall be condemned to be bound and put alive into a sack and choked in water, and thereafter, that her dead body be brought to a place of execution and placed on a pole as an example and mirror to others'. The sentence, however, was only whipping and banishment from the city for life. Barbara Adriaens paid for her marriages each time with exile from the city where she was living, and of the first time we know that she owed this light punishment to the intervention of a visiting French duchess, who took interest in her case. In Cornelia Gerritse's case a lesbian relationship was evident, but no mention was made of sodomy in the verdict. Her case was exceptional in that her 'spouse', who was equally guilty but who lived as a woman, was given the same sentence of twelve years exile from Leiden.

It was not so much lesbian relationships or cross-dressing in and of themselves, but their combination, that was considered to be extremely serious. We can also conclude that the one of two female lovers who assumed the role of the man was as a rule more severely punished than her accomplice. The attempted usurpation of the male prerogative was not dismissed lightly. It is also striking that the courts were very hesitant in pressing the charge or even suggesting the existence of sodomy, and that whereas the judges knew and agreed that the death penalty was prescribed for sodomy, the courts were considerably reluctant to put this into practice.

OFFICERS IN THE FLEET AND ARMY

The ship's surgeon De Graaff described how quickly tensions arose after a discovery of a disguised woman among a male community who sometimes saw no women for months on the long trip to the East. Such a discovery caused a considerable amount of trouble to captains and officers, who had no choice but to take immediate action. Despite this, we found no negative evidence concerning the manner in which the unmasked female soldiers or sailors did their work. They generally received the wages they had earned and sometimes more than that. Among the papers of Admiral Tromp, we found a 'Document Concerning Seamen Become Female Persons'. This concerned Jannetje Pieters and Aeltje Jans who had entered the service of the VOC. When war broke out with England in 1653, they were pressed into the navy. In this document, the captain of their ship was requested to 'remand them (= the women) at the earliest possible moment and in the most civil manner to their lords and masters and to give them certificates of good conduct in order that they might be paid their wages as it had been found that they had observed their positions in a fitting and proper manner and had comported themselves well'. Their captain certainly judged them positively and they were therefore properly paid.

As far as we have the information, the unmasked female sailors of the other sea wars were also judged favourably and well treated. We know of two who did not have to repay their earnest-money, and another who received travel money when she was put off the ship. Cases also occurred in which the rights to collect booty and sickness monies were honoured.

Illustrative of the responsibilities of the authorities in such cases is the story of Maritgen Jans, about whom we are rather well-informed. Maritgen Jans, who had served as a soldier in a West Indies Company fort in Africa, and who had done her work there well, was discovered when she fell ill and had to be nursed in a hospital. The Governor immediately had a separate room made ready for her, wanting to send her back to Holland at the first opportunity – for what else could he do with a single white woman among all those men, so far from the fatherland? The only alternative was that she should marry as soon as possible, so he would no longer be responsible for her; we have seen the same reaction in the case of Maria Elisabeth Meening. Maritgen herself did not want to go back to Holland, so a marriage was organised for her, and this proceeded in a most efficient fashion. First, women's clothing were ordered for her. The Governor and the council gave her a golden chain, a beautiful frock and other presents with the express purpose to make her a more desirable bride. A number of candidates quickly reported themselves ready to fill the position of husband, and these were permitted to visit her at her sick-bed and talk to her 'in order to see if some love could come of it'. Maritgen eventually chose a 35-year old jurist, a much better match than she could ever have achieved in Holland.

The wedding took place only three weeks after the discovery and was celebrated with much ostentation and festivities lasting for four days, with all the customs observed. The Governor performed the function of father of the bride. He declared that this solution had been dictated to him by the Lord. It proved, alas, a short-lived one, as the groom fell prey to a tropical illness a few weeks later and died. Maritgen was then sent back to the fatherland at the first opportunity.

PUBLIC OPINION AND POPULAR SONGS

As female cross-dressing was a living tradition among the common folk, it would be logical to expect a certain degree of toleration for women who dressed as men. But we found very little indication of this. Toleration, however, tends to leave fewer traces in the archives than its opposite. In only two cases did we find proof of some acceptance within a small circle. One example is that of a woman in a Dutch village, who went through life with the significant name, 'Aart de Broekman' (*broek* = trousers), and who was employed as a farm worker. Her cross-dressing was apparently accepted, but came to an end because a new maidservant on the farm where Aart worked refused to share a bed with 'him'. This servant protested to the church council which as a result insisted to the village council that Aart must dress 'as sacred and human laws entail'. The local court put the choice to Aart: leave or dress as a woman. We do not know her choice. The second example, that of Maria van Antwerpen, was restricted to the family. One of her brothers and his wife appeared as godfather and godmother for the child that she, as 'father', had baptised in Amsterdam.

There are hints that other members of Maria van Antwerpen's family and acquaintances knew of her cross-dressing. For example, when she was later living as a man under the name of Machiel van Handtwerpen, she visited her former landlady in Gouda, which implies that the latter knew of her secret. Moreover, in the same town Maria dressed as an 'amazon' for some time while living there as a woman, by which we suppose that she dressed in men's clothing but was nonetheless recognisable as a woman. It is also clear from what we know of Barbara Adriaens, Maritgen Jans, Geertruida van den Heuvel and others, that there often were intimates who knew, or had discovered, the true sex, but who, for some reason and sometimes temporarily, kept their mouths shut.

But knowledge can not always be taken as acceptance and toleration, or as an indication of a favourable judgement.

However, we found positive reactions with regard to some female cross-dressers who had resumed life as women after a period as man. This was particularly the case when their military or naval careers had been successful, no further misdeeds had been committed, and they had become ordinary, respected female citizens. Then they could even become popular and local celebrities. The ex-soldier Margareta of Groningen profited from this, for example, by opening a shop. The ex-sailor and soldier, Aagt de Tamboer (*tamboer* = drummer), in Amsterdam in the seventeenth century attracted customers to her inn by hanging a signpost with the following text on it:

> Here Aagt de Tamboer dwells
> That which she does, she does it well
> Twice as tar with Tromp she sailed
> But still is sound of limb and hale
> She swims as well as fish or whale
> Lately, she saved a drowning lass
> The cost to see her: a mug or glass!

In contrast, a great many women encountered first reactions which were hostile and aggressive. Immediately after signing on as a sailor, Lena Wasmoet was discovered and subjected to the *maling*, which meant that she was surrounded by a crowd of people who pushed and jostled her, a form of popular justice which occurred regularly in the streets of Amsterdam.[6] The arrest of Barbara Adriaens also was accompanied by angry crowds, and the police only just saved her from the *maling*. And, more so in the seventeenth than in the eighteenth century, this hostility could survive the first confrontation. The life of Hendrickje Lamberts, whom the neighbourhood knew had served as a soldier in the past, was so embittered by it, as she stated in her trial, 'that she never dared take to the streets for the harassment of the people'.

Maria van Antwerpen provides us with the most detailed impressions concerning the reaction to those whose cross-dressing was abruptly discovered. As she was brought into Breda after her arrest, half the inhabitants of the city lined the roads to look and laugh. Remarks were directed at her wife, who had also been arrested, such as 'How many children have you had of Jan van Ant?' While in prison, Maria was the centre of attention and interest. 'The throng of people was so great at the main entrance that the guards could not obstruct them, and each was enrapt with astonishment about such a rare case. They asked me thousands of questions, and I had heavy work to satisfy their curiosity. It fell happily to my lot to be allowed to remain there a day longer, and the beneficence of the military and civil persons was very great. (. . .). That afternoon I was brought drinks from all sides . . . such that when I was brought in the evening to the house of the captain master-at-arms, I was quite befuddled. The rush of people was then so abundant that it was necessary for each of us to conduct two separate watches thereafter . . . '.

These first reactions can be summed up as astonishment, hilarity, curiosity, but no real hostility was involved. In Maria's case, the negative aspects (she was married to a woman) and the positive (she had served valiantly as a soldier) were balanced. Moreover, it seems that in the second half of the eighteenth century the judgement became increasingly less harsh and fierce. That is, at any rate, a tendency we can see in popular songs.

Reactions and opinions among the lower classes of society are not easy to find, but in addition to trial records one other rich source does exist: song books. Popular songs played an important role in the daily life of the common people, and they were sung in the streets, in inns, at fairs and at work. Songs served not only as entertainment but also as a source of news and to shape political opinion. News about war and peace, events in local or national politics and in particular about grisly murders, horrible accidents and strange occurrences were quickly reflected in songs. The texts, with an indication of the melody to which they should be sung, were offered for sale by the singers to bystanders. These street singers and news peddlars came from the marginal groups of society, even though we might expect some degree of literacy, and they were often treated like vagabonds. Criminal records show that many of them were women.

Loose sheets of songs were often bound into song books which were sold in book shops or hawked about. Many such song books have been preserved, and these, moreover, can be complemented by what has been recorded from the oral tradition in our century.[7] In view of the public for which these folk songs were intended, we can consider these as a deposit of information reflecting the opinion of the common people.

In these collections of songs, we found more than thirty with the theme of female cross-dressing. Most of these were noted down in the eighteenth and nineteenth centuries, but many must have been later versions of earlier songs, and some actually date from the seventeenth century.

In view of the sensation usually caused by the discovery of a disguised women, many of these songs probably originally functioned as news songs. It is, however, often difficult to find evidence concerning the historical events upon which they were based. As a rule, the singers presenting the events described them as if they had just occurred, putting considerable effort into embellishing them with local colour. This makes it all the more difficult to determine which case is concerned. A song which was published as 'The remarkable story of a maidservant by the name of Anna Katrijn who encountered misfortune while in service and, at a recruiter's in the Vinkestraat in Amsterdam, accordingly resolved to sail to the East Indies as a sailor', sounds very credible because of the concrete details provided, until one discovers that another version exists in which the maidservant is called Anna Maria, and in which she enlisted in the Bredestraat in Rotterdam.[8] The best remembered song with this theme is *Daar was laatst een meisje loos*, cited in the Introductory chapter, which has come down to us in several versions. In one of the oldest the heroine's name is Margriet van Dijk and the ship upon which she was to have sailed was called *De Eik*. But we could not find either Margriet or *De Eik* in the archives.[9]

As a rule, the singers loved to embellish their stories, and they gave special attention to sexual and other salient details. If these details did not exist, they were invented; we can establish this in cases for which we know something about the women concerned. Comparing the facts with the image presented helps us interpreting the songs. It is, for example, noteworthy that in the songs, the women were often described as having been sentenced to a harsher punishment than they had been in reality, and the opinion of the singer is always that they fully deserved what they got. Hostility, scorn and hilarity were the reactions most often found in the songs, especially the older ones. The sexual aspects were dwelt upon rather coarsely and with considerable malicious pleasure. Women were described as very eager for sex. The idea that sex was possible without a penis, or that a woman might attempt to marry another woman without having this irreplaceable attribute at her disposal was considered the height of absurdity. We already cited a song in which a female sailor acquired an artificial penis of horn. In a song about Maria van Antwerpen, a scene is described which was to have taken place in the nuptial bed. The bride is told:

> Without mast, I sail
> And cannot avail
> Me of what thou desires

This clearly had its origin in fantasy, as Maria van Antwerpen's first spouse did not know the true sex of her 'husband'. Sometimes however, the singers did not have to supplement reality. The following lines were written about Barbara Adriaens and Hilletje Jans, who married in Amsterdam in 1632:

> For when the bride made free
> To feel if there might be
> cock and balls, said she,
> 'T' is most rare
> I perceive them not, yea, nothing there,
> How may I then assay
> My heat with thee thus to allay
> In the nuptial bed where we two lay[10]

This passage conforms more or less literally – albeit in a poetic form – with what Hilletje Jans told the court.

The negative view taken in the songs about cross-dressing women, especially if they had usurped the male privilege of courting women is not only apparent in the tone of the descriptions, but is also directly stated. 'A new song of two females who married in the *Nieuwe Kerk* in Amsterdam' is one of the songs made up about Cornelia Gerrits and Elisabeth Boleyn, who married in Amsterdam in 1685. It begins as follows:

> Listen, friends, to my tale
> Of how two jades their duties failed
> They did abandon the lawful bed
> Of the men that they had wed
> To flee, and these wives are now
> Themselves bound by the marriage vow

The song then goes on to describe how Cornelia, dressed in men's clothing, met her lawful husband from whom she had been separated nine years before in Leiden:

> He did inspect her, foot to head
> And spoke thus, 'Beast, to walk the street,
> I shall see thee snared in dread
> Thy evil paid, thy justice mete

According to this song, they were sent to prison for this, while in fact they were exiled. They were described to be:

> Arrested in a trice
> And taken to gaol
> Where they ceaselessly rail
> Against marriage and vice
> The deed that they mourn
> And life's lot of scorn[11]

In a song entitled, 'Of a female brought to jail who there must sew and spin with a hat on her head and a jerkin on her back'. We recognize Trijn Jurriaens, who indeed in 1679 was sentenced to serve her prison's term in men's clothing. It ends in the following way:

> The sentence must be praised
> (. . .) Who will, approach and stay
> To look, to marvel at a man
> Once comely, kindly, grand
> (. . .) Become a curious display[12]

Another song about an unidentified woman in The Hague ends with the following lines:

> Let Sir Bawd in prison spin
> I have no pity for her, no;
> Who doth with such sport begin
> Begins in sport and ends in woe[13]

These songs corroborate the notion that it was precisely among the common folk that the greatest disapproval of these women existed. And in the few cases for which another tone can be detected, there is also little evidence of understanding of or sympathy for such women. In more comic songs, the main character is often a girl who cannot find a lover on land and then disguises herself as a soldier or sailor in order to satisfy her sexual needs, as in a song about three women who enlisted during the Dutch Revolt. They did so because of 'amorous heat' and 'to go drinking'. They quickly squandered their earnest-money' whereupon their officers discovered their real sex:

> They laughed aloud at them there
> And a sentence did declare[14]

According to the songs, the ordinary soldiers and sailors did not have such strong objections, because they considered females discovered on board ship to be fair game. In one seaman's ballad, in which it is explicitly claimed that it was written by a common sailor, we read that after the discovery of a disguised female, the sailors wished:

> That half the ship's crew might be so
> That they might go
> Rutting at sea
> With fifty lasses as fine as she[15]

Remarkably enough, a positive response can be found in a song about a female sailor who was discovered to be a woman by two Spaniards who boarded her ship and then attempted to rape her. For her bravery in holding these two foreigners at bay with a knife, she was praised and rewarded:

> Thus the Admiral Supreme
> And Gentlemen did speak
> Thou didst not our praises seek
> But worthy we do find thee
> Hadst thou killed them with thy blade
> Even without needs be
> Thou hadst thy virtue thus preserved
> And art a stalward, dapper maid
> And herewith we commend thee[16]

As a reward, she was given a house, an inn and a husband, at least in the song. In this, we can recognise patterns which we also encountered in reality. Cross-dressing could be permissible so long as the woman claimed no masculine prerogatives, maintained her feminine honour, was extremely successful as a man, and finally resumed life as a woman in the end.

After 1800, the tradition of female transvestism dwindled fast. But songs about such women were sung until late in the nineteenth century, however, especially in Flanders. But the songs sung in the late eighteenth and the nineteenth centuries differed noticeably from the earlier ones. The songs from the northern Netherlands sung in the seventeenth and eighteenth centuries as a rule concern female sailors or are news songs about sensational cases such as that of Barbara Adriaens. The motives attributed to the disguised women were reprehensible – they sought an easy way to acquire money; they had pretentions of becoming male; it seemed a clever way to catch a man – and the tone is extremely negative. In the second half of the eighteenth and nineteenth centuries, the heroines are often soldiers, a development to which the great Napoleonic wars contributed. The tone, however, had become quite different, and one can find considerable admiration in them for the heroic women. This is clear even in a version of a song about Maria van Antwerpen dating from the early nineteenth century:

> Valorious in manner
> Stout-hearted in blood
> Moral and honourable
> Steadfast of nerve

This is quite different from the judgement made of Barbara Adriaens, who was arrested for the same offence more than a century earlier:

> In appearance and in dress
> An indignity to her sex

Cross-dressing women who seduced members of their own sex disappeared from the songs as they did from reality. The motives imputed to the women in these later songs are also positive: patriotism, and, in particular, the desire to follow a lover or husband. Such songs often ended on the battlefield, where he saved her, or she him. Sometimes one or both were killed; sometimes the song ended with a marital reunion or a marriage, as was the case in a Dutch song about a French female soldier:

> Her valour was acclaimed by all
> And the Council did agree
> That these two might be
> By the marriage vow united
> And to remain thus undivided
> And so in the hangman's stead
> The priest was called
> And the two were wed[17]

The nineteenth-century songs were increasingly less concerned with the reality of the old tradition. Further, the language used became more and more decent. In short, these songs drifted increasingly into the genre of romantic fictitious tearjerkers.

DIFFERENCES BETWEEN COMMON FOLK AND THE ÉLITE

If these songs comprise a source whereby we may learn something about the opinions of the common folk, we must look elsewhere for insight into the notions of the literate middle and upper classes. References to and commentaries on cases of female cross-dressing can be found in chronicles, diaries, travel narratives, collections of anecdotes, popular scientific treatises, daily newspapers and magazines. These sources yield many mixed but also a considerable number of purely positive reactions. We find references to historical and classical mythological figures, such as Joan of Arc and the Amazons. In the mythical and legendary tradition of the theme, heroism and the preservation of virginity were important criteria. Pieter de Lange, the author of a seventeenth-century collection of anecdotes, for example, placed the two female sailors about whom he was writing, in the tradition of the amazons, praising them because they 'preferred an honourable death to a life of shame'.

Opinions concerning female cross-dressing fell readily into the heated literary debate of these centuries concerning the nature of women. It was no coincidence that the seventeenth century witnessed a boom in the number of publications concerning Pope Joan. She was the woman, who, according to legend, was elected Pope in the ninth century while disguised in men's – or to be more precise – monk's clothing. This discussion culminated in a book by Frederic Spanheim, printed in Leiden in 1691, in which nearly 500 works which had appeared since the thirteenth century concerning this mythic figure were critically examined. His book was repeatedly reprinted and was also published in abridged editions in French and German.[18]

In the Netherlands, the famous and influential doctor, Johannes van Beverwijk took up the *querelle des femmes* with verve. In 1639, he published his book *On the Excellence of Women*, in which he listed a number of Dutch female soldiers, praising their courageous deeds. Positive opinions from chronicle writers in the seventeenth century include those of Caspar Ens and Nicolaas van Wassenaer, among others.

Chronicles and newspapers naturally paid most attention to recent and sensational cases, and they did not restrict themselves to the Dutch Republic. The popular monthly, *Europische Mercurius*, for example, reported in 1749 that the executioner of Lyon who had performed more than sixty executions had inadvertently betrayed herself while in a drunken state to be a woman.[19] That same journal commented in 1727 positively, although somewhat ironically, on a case in England of cross-dressing which included a marriage between two women. But some years later, the conduct of Maria van Antwerpen was described by them as 'unnatural and illegal', and further that 'such brutish women' were deserving the death penalty. This diversity is characteristic of the greater ambivalence to be found among the higher classes.[20] Still, fundamentally, the judgement expressed concerning these women was predominantly negative for this strata as well, the more so when it happened close to home.

In moralistic works from the seventeenth and eighteenth centuries, we find warnings against cross-dressing based upon the Biblical text in Deuteronomy.[21] It was a clergyman who, after Barbara Adriaens' arrest in Amsterdam in 1632, pressed for the pronouncement of the death penalty for her crimes. Jacob van de Vivere is a good example of ambiguity. In his popular collection of anecdotes, first printed in 1615, he wrote that he admired the courage of female soldiers, but at the same time admitted that he disliked courageous women, deeming them rather ridiculous. He evoked the Bible to justify his rejection of them.[22] In Simon de Vries, a writer of many popular scientific and sensational works in the second half of the seventeenth century, we find a similar ambivalence about our women. On the one hand, one finds admiration for their brave deeds in his works, but on the other hand, he also condemns them for their cross-dressing: 'Such women are in no way praiseworthy who deny their sex so that they may follow the war in men's clothing, fine though their deeds may have been.' He conceded, however: 'It cannot be denied that honour is due such (women).'[23] Ridicule was also among the reactions of the elite; we know that among the upper circles of The Hague, a joke circulated around 1670 about a 'tribas' which was based upon the case of Barbara Adriaens or Hendrickje Verschuur.[24]

Among those writers whose opinions were unambiguously

negative concerning such women, we find precisely those who came into closest contact with them. The ship's surgeon Nicolaus de Graaff is one example; and Nicolaas Tulp, who condemned cross-dressing women fiercely in his *Observationum medicarum* served as a magistrate in the trial of Hendrickje Verschuur.

CROSS-DRESSING IN LITERATURE

In the seventeenth and eighteenth centuries, a growing flood of popular prose streamed from the Dutch printing presses, the majority of which was directed at the middle classes. The greater proportion of these were early novels, and more-or-less fictional autobiographies. A detailed, but certainly not complete, bibliography of popular Dutch prose from the years 1600–1815 includes twenty-five works on the subject, nearly all of which concern cross-dressing by women.[25] The first novel on this theme dates from 1624, but most were published in the eighteenth century, when such novels developed into a genre of their own. The theme was considered attractive, because, as we read in the introduction to one of the works, 'it is well known that the strangest occurrences may happen to those whose sex and clothing are incompatible'.[26]

Some of these works were purely fictitious; others were based upon reality. The ghost-written autobiography of Maria van Antwerpen could be proved to adhere very closely to the facts. Another biography entitled *De vrouwelyke soldaat* ('The female soldier'), which appeared shortly after 1743, is also probably quite trustworthy. The author, indicated only with the initials, M. T. M., can be identified as Maria ter Meetelen. We were able to trace her in the archives. Unfortunately, the episode describing her life as a soldier is short; the book is particularly interesting and historically important because of the description of her experiences as a prisoner in North Africa. We have more doubts about the authenticity of the autobiography of Maria Kinkons which appeared in 1759. She was to have had adventures while dressed as a man both on land and at sea. But the only information we could prove as historic was the name of the ship on which she presumably had sailed. But this is insufficient to include this work among the authentic stories.[27]

A large number of other works are clearly fictitious, as the adventures are too fantastic and the heroines' names too exotic.

The fictional autobiography was a favourite form for the novel at the time, and this fact must make us all the more cautious, particularly as one sometimes encounters real incidents and characters in otherwise fictional works. The discovery in 1743 of a woman who had worked as stableboy in Amsterdam for years led, for example, to one or two semi-fictional works. It is sometimes not possible to determine the degree to which fiction or reality is involved, however, as in the case of the 'Stout-Hearted Heroine', which we have discussed before. We believe that this is partly fiction, despite the fact that this book pretends to reflect reality, and the introduction even stresses the fact that many books have appeared concerning women dressed as men 'which are not true in all details'. On the other hand, the sketch provided in the book of what life as a man was like can be more readily termed realistic than fantastic, and it may thus serve as an historical source nonetheless.

Also, just as in the songs, it is remarkable that the more fictional the nature of the works in question, the more the tone and judgement concerning the women tended to be laudatory. The women are depicted as real 'heroines' – although some irony can be detected in this classification. Franciscus Kersteman, Maria van Antwerpen's ghost writer, who in his autobiography admitted that he had earned a considerable sum by 'The Heroine of Breda' in later years also wrote a few travesty novels, each of which was more positive in tone and contained wilder adventures than Maria's autobiography. He also conveyed this idea of making money to his brother, who tried his hand at this genre, too.[28]

The popularity of the theme of female cross-dressing was not limited to the Republic; it was a general European phenomenon. References in chronicles, magazines, collections of anecdotes and the like can be found in Italy, Spain, France, and England, as well as folk songs and, especially, more-or-less fictional (auto)biographies concerning such women. The notion that the theme was not limited by national boundaries is supported too by the number of translations which appeared. We found Dutch translations of French biographies, like those of Christine de Meirak and Renée Bordereau, and of the English ones of Anna Blound, Henriette de Boston and Hannah Snell. The biography of Catarina Vizzani was translated from Italian into English, and that of Géneviève Prémoy was translated from French into Dutch as well as English – to give a few examples only.[29]

The theme of female cross-dressing was equally popular in the theatre. Cross-dressing in dramatic performances, however, was a complicated matter, because it was originally common practice for men to play women's roles.[30] Only in 1655 did a woman join the permanent company of the Amsterdam Theatre. Quite apart from this, however, cross-dressing was presented on stage quite frequently as an integral part of the work being performed. Cross-dressing by men as well as women was presented. In farces, it was often the man in women's clothing who provoked hilarity, but in what was perhaps the most popular Dutch comedy of the seventeenth century, *Nieuwsgierig Aagje* ('Miss Inquisitive') a drunken woman is dressed in men's clothing as a joke.[31] Female cross-dressing was popular in the theatre in other countries as well. Of more than three hundred plays first performed in London between 1660 and 1700, eighty-nine contained roles in which actresses donned male clothes.[32]

Apart from making the idea of female cross-dressing more conceivable to a larger audience than that reached by the printed prose works of the time, the theatrical and real-life tradition of the theme reinforced each other in other ways as well. We already referred to Dutch actresses who preferred men's clothing to women's garb in their daily lives, as well as on the stage: non-Dutch examples are Madame de Maupin in France and Charlotte Charke in England.[33] The latter, characteristically enough, produced a theatre play about Pope Joan. More than once, reality gave rise to a drama, such as those about the Spaniard Catalina de Erauso and the Englishwoman Mary Frith.[34] The opposite also occurred. It was said of a singer in the Paris opera in 1724 that she had served five or six years with the Dutch troops.[35] Hannah Snell, after a successful career as a sailor, staged a revue about her life as a man – for her, myth and reality were no longer divisible.[36]

Painters and draughtsmen have found their inspirations in the theme to a much lesser extent. We know of only one authentic print of a Dutch female soldier, that of Geertruid ten Brugge, which dates from the beginning of the eighteenth century. This woman had been a soldier for some time, but had later resumed life as a woman in The Hague. There, unmarried, she bore a child in 1706. In the baptismal records, she is registered as 'La Dragonne'. She was apparently a local celebrity and possibly earned money selling copies of this print. Exploitation of fame is a characteristic we have encountered before and was also not exclusively Dutch.

The greatest number of images we have of female cross-dressers come from illustrations from books which dealt with such women. The Dutch edition of the autobiography of Hannah Snell, for example, included illustrations which may not have copied reality, but which in any case give us some insight into how artists imagined such women. Generally, they tried to render male as well as female traits simultaneously, so that the viewer could see at a glance that a disguised woman was being depicted. For these reasons, if for no other, these prints may not be termed realistic.

This was also the case for prints which constituted a genre in itself, namely those with the themes of 'the world turned upside down' and 'women on top', or 'the battle of the trousers'.[37] In these folk prints, dating mostly from the sixteenth century but reprinted as children's gifts until the beginning of the nineteenth century, all sorts of anomalies were, cartoonlike, depicted as a warning to the viewer. Next to drawings such as 'The servant strikes his master', 'The man carries his horse' or; 'The fish sit in the trees', one always finds prints such as 'The woman goes to war'. The changing of gender roles was a frequent feature in such prints, because it confused the 'natural order of things'. A very distinctive print culture existed in the early modern period in the Netherlands, Germany and elsewhere concerning the theme 'the women don trousers', in which fear and rejection of women who coveted the position of males was made abundantly plain. The message in all these prints is clear: chaos threatens the world when the separate spheres of the sexes are confused.

CONTACTS WITH ROYALTY

In histories of female soldiers and sailors, a theme repeatedly emerges in which they are received at court and rewarded. These usually concerned women who were to have begun cross-dressing out of patriotism and loyalty to their sovereign. When such women bore their arms in an exemplary fashion on the battlefield a royal gesture of pardon and reward was in order. Maybe this can be placed in the tradition of interest of monarchs for human curiosities like dwarves, but female soldiers certainly had a propaganda value: the monarch could show to the world that even women rallied under his banners.

An example from the beginning of the seventeenth century

presents the Spanish woman Catalina de Erauso, who was given a pension from Philip IV. She was also received by the Pope, who is said to have given her permission to continue wearing men's clothing.[38] This recognition came after a life as a conquistador in South America, where she not only had not behaved like a lady, but in fact not like a gentleman either. In England, Queen Anne and King George IV extended favours to various cross-dressers. The English ex-soldiers, 'Christian Davis', Phoebe Hessel and Mary Anne Talbot, were to have lived from money that they received directly from high nobles and from the king himself.[39] The last in this series is the German Antoinette Berg, who in English service fought the French on Dutch territory in 1799. During the peace festivities in London in 1814 she was even presented to the Tsar of Russia and the King of Prussia.[40] France provided its own examples, from Louis XIV, who rewarded his soldier Géneviève Prémoy with a fine pension and a knighthood in the order of St. Louis,[41] to Napoleon, who was to have bestowed the Legion of Honour to the Flemish Maria Schellinck in 1808.[42]

The Netherlands were a Republic, but for the greater part of the seventeenth and eighteenth centuries, the offices of Stadhouder and commander-in-chief of the army and fleet were hereditary within the House of Orange. The Stadhouders could therefore be – and were at the time – compared to monarchs in other European countries. And indeed we did find examples of their rewarding female soldiers and sailors, especially connected with Stadhouder Willem III, the later King William of England. He was to have given Elisabeth Sommuruell an annuity of 200 guilders for her valour as a soldier during the war with France in 1672–78. Newspapers tell us that he received Willempje Gerrits at his court. In 'The Stout-Hearted Heroine' this story is also told, and this royal treatment there also included 'Hendrik van den Berg'.[43] Later, as King of England, Willem awarded a pension to a woman in men's clothing, the soldier 'Robert Cornelius', in 1696.[44]

Maria van Antwerpen wrote in her autobiography that she had hoped to complete her six years of service and then to make a triumphant revelation of her sex and reap benefits from it. This idea can easily have been inspired by stories about Elisabeth Sommuruell, who, like her, came from Breda. At Maria's second trial in 1769, answering the question why she had disobeyed the stipulations made at her former trial, she declared that she had been received by Willem IV in 1751 and that he had personally granted her a pardon, reversing the sentence she had received earlier that year. As 'guarantee' she had been given a golden medallion upon which the image and weapon of Willem were engraved. Unfortunately, she could not prove it as she had sold the coin when in need of money. She swore that the medallion had been seen by many people, but the judges attached little value to this story. We do not know whether to believe her either, as the archives where an answer might have been found, have been lost by now.

But in a news song which circulated about her the following lines were included, proving, if nothing else, how important this royal reward was to the popular imagination.

> The Prince of Orange
> Granted a pardon
> Freed by her Sovereign
> She came out of prison

The theme emerges in many ballads throughout Europe. A song about a fictitious woman who was to have fought on the Dutch side during the Belgian Revolt in 1830 for example runs

> (She) did the Cross of Honour earn
> When of her loyal deeds
> The Crown Prince learned.[45]

In reality, this kind of royal reward was the exception and should in some cases be taken with a pinch of salt. But it is clear that the contact between the monarchy and such women appealed to the common folk. Although female cross-dressers and the monarchs had little in common in real life, they both appealed to the popular imagination and so they found each other in the myths created around them.

CONCLUSION

These contacts with royalty show a reaction that can be called positive. But when we sum up contemporary reactions, we must conclude that the basic judgement passed on cross-dressing women was negative. We found very little indication of toleration, other than in novels and plays. Women who had been successful as soldiers or sailors, who could give acceptable motives for living as men and who subsequently resumed respectable life as a woman were sometimes positively received. However, more often the sensational or comic aspect of cross-dressing set the tone. Rejection was the most common reaction, and it is remarkable that among the common folk this was generally much more pronounced than among the elite, where fewer black-and-white judgements were made. The relatively more negative position generally taken by the common folk is puzzling as the tradition of female transvestism was rooted in this very social stratum. But then, we do not know if the street songs and behaviour of the crowds did fully express the feelings of the women present. We can only guess that deep in their hearts some of them must have understood.

6
Some Conclusions

In her memoirs published in 1924, Aletta Jacobs described how, in 1870, when she was fifteen years old, she was seized with horror at the idea of having to dedicate her entire life to housework. She fantasised eagerly that she would flee home and, dressed as a boy, sign on to a ship, and sail to America, to become a coachman there.[1] But in 1870, it would have been most unusual to put this idea into practice. Little remained in nineteenth-century Holland of what had been a flourishing tradition of female cross-dressing in the seventeenth and eighteenth centuries. In other European countries this tradition vanished as well.[2] For women like Aletta Jacobs, who was the daughter of a country surgeon, other pathways gradually opened up. She was the first woman to be given the right to study at a Dutch university, and became Holland's first female doctor and most celebrated feminist.

The 119 cases of female cross-dressing between 1550 and 1839 described in this book show that in former times it was not at all exceptional for women to take on the appearance of men as a solution to their personal problems. And, in spite of differences, these women can in many ways be described as one group. They were young women from the lower classes in society, and generally had a background of rootlessness caused by the death of one or both parents, family quarrels, or migration. Many of them were not born in the Netherlands, most were single and alone. They all encountered the same difficulties in the practical side of their gender change, and in the problems of maintaining themselves in a men's world. The way in which most of them were discovered also showed many similarities. It is in the personal motives that we find most variety, but here also fixed patterns can be discerned. Destitution was a stimulus for many, sometimes in combination with the wish to follow or remain with husband, lover, or family. Some were full of patriotic fervour when their country was at war. Others used cross-dressing as a disguise when fleeing home or a husband, or for easing a criminal career. Deeper-seated motives of a psychological or sexual nature must have played a decisive role in many cases. In particular, cross-dressing gave women who were in love with other women psychologically the freedom to enter into actual sexual relations. Before the end of the eighteenth century the expression of love between two women usually took the form of the imitation of a normal, often even married heterosexual couple. Female cross-dressing has therefore been an important stage in the development of female homosexuality.

Whatever the personal motives for dressing as a man, an important consideration was that the women knew that they had predecessors, that other women had made the same decision. Popular songs recounted adventures of female sailors and soldiers, and, even if they were mostly negative and derisive in tone, some of them also told how brave women were rewarded and even received by their sovereign. The fact that temporary cross-dressing was a regular element at festivities and a common theme in folklore, must have influenced the women and strengthened the tradition.

Contemporaries of higher classes were very well aware of the phenomenon, in the Netherlands and elsewhere. Handbooks for notaries discussed the question of the validity of acts which had been passed in the presence of male witnesses who later turned out to be women in disguise.[3] In 1762, an Englishman jestingly wrote that there were so many disguised women in the army, that it would be better to create separate regiments for them.[4] Another eighteenth-century English author, John Addison, more seriously noted that it would be interesting to make a list of female cross-dressers.[5] Presumably, we are the first to follow this suggestion.

Female cross-dressing was often treated in the press. The lives of many such women found their way into books, which were published in the Netherlands, England, France, Spain, Italy, North America, and which have been repeatedly translated from one language to another. Female cross-dressers apparently exercised a strong fascination over the reading public, although these readers came from the middle and upper classes, and so had a social background quite different from that of the women herself. In the eighteenth century the theme of cross-dressing was very popular in fictional novels too, whereas it is supposed that women formed the majority of those who read novels; this can be taken as an indication that the idea of female cross-dressing appealed to women of middle and upper classes also, although few of them actually took to this road.

In spite of the popularity of the theme, reactions to real-life transvestism were fundamentally negative. It was forbidden in the Bible, and it also confused the social order and threatened the hierarchy of the sexes; ambiguity on the matter of gender presumably made people ill at ease. However, a few women who had successful careers as sailors and soldiers and who had resumed respectable lives as women met with praise and reward. Successful female soldiers or sailors were sometimes even granted exceptional favours from monarchs, or, in the case of the Dutch Republic, the *Stadhouders*. These contacts with royalty belong both to the myth and the reality of female cross-dressing.

On the other hand, it is true that a remarkable number of female cross-dressers associated with criminals. The crossing of the barrier between the sexes obviously eased the transgression of other norms, and vice versa. Of course, cross-dressing in itself had a subversive character: it turned the social order upside down. Men occupied a position in the social hierarchy above that of women, and it was felt that women who passed as men usurped male prerogatives in a fraudulent manner.

In the seventeenth and eighteenth century, the theme of cross-dressing emerged frequently in theatre performances, novels, songs, prints, and other forms of cultural expression. Sometimes these expressions were intended as admonitions, and then the image depicted was negative; sometimes the presentation was positive. In folksongs we often find condemnation, and malicious delight in the women's downfall, whereas in the novels a more positive presentation dominated. From this, it can be seen that it was precisely among the common people – from whose midst the women themselves came – that strong disapproval existed. However, from the second half of the eighteenth century on, the popular songs became more praising and more romantic in tone. Lastly, it appeared as a rule that the greater the fictional element, the milder the reaction.

All these songs, novels and other expressions of the theme certainly influenced real-life transvestism. Oral tradition and written texts must have provided the initial idea, and gave the women models to follow. The interplay between myth and reality as well as the important aspect of role-playing is clearly demonstrated in the fact that many actresses who played trouser-roles on the stage preferred to dress in men's clothing in their daily lives. The other side of this is, that several former cross-dressers took to the stage.

Although female cross-dressers could be found all over Europe, it was in the north-west that the vast majority of them lived. In these parts the late age of marriage for women, the relatively great freedom accorded to them, and customary female migration patterns, put young lower-class women in real risk of finding themselves destitute and friendless far from home. It should not surprise us further that Holland and England produced and attracted most of these women, as they were seafaring and warring nations, who could use any supply of untrained sailors and soldiers. In France, we see a sudden boom in female soldiers in the revolutionary armies at the end of the eighteenth century. The Mediterranean countries in general did not produce many female cross-dressers. Young women were generally less free and also more protected there.

Female transvestism as a phenomenon clearly was concentrated in the seventeenth and eighteenth centuries. In the Netherlands, only three cases are known for the sixteenth century. We cannot be absolutely certain that the boom in female cross-dressing only began in the late sixteenth century, as it is in theory possible that cross-dressing was tolerated before that time and that no attention was paid to such women. The theme of cross-dressing was certainly older in folklore, and traces could also be found in Medieval hagiography of female saints who resorted to a male disguise. Still, it is very unlikely that writers and authorities would have had nothing to say about such a remarkable phenomenon. The thesis of the origination of the tradition of female cross-dressing in the sixteenth century can, however, be related to the postponement of the age of marriage, the widespread migration and the quickly growing demand for sailors and soldiers which were also features of that age.

The disappearance of the tradition in the nineteenth century is not surprising. The growing bureaucracy created ever more obstacles for women in disguise, in the form of Civil Registration, enforced military service, and medical examinations. The story of Francina Gunningh Sloet, told in Chapter 4, clearly demonstrates that after 1800 it was beginning to be difficult to travel without official papers of identification. Moreover, for a number of women cross-dressing had lost its function, because as a means of entering into a relationship with another woman it was quickly becoming anachronistic. The declining attraction of cross-dressing to women can also be related to changes in the relationship between men and women around 1800. Before the nineteenth century, this relationship was first and foremost hierarchical: the man above the woman. In the dominant ideology, from the late eighteenth century onwards, the gender roles became more complementary: man and woman stood side-by-side, each complementing the other out of his or her own sphere of life.[6] In this context, putting on men's clothes by women no longer raised women upwards to a higher status, while, by contrast, more men dared to dress in women's clothes. Moreover, after 1800, the Netherlands no longer offered a good matrix for female transvestism. The country had lost much of its attraction to immigrants, the VOC was dead and buried, and Holland entered a long period of economic decline – and peace.

The disappearance of female cross-dressing ran in parallel with its disappearance from cultural expressions. Folk songs with this theme retained their popularity longest, but only *Daar was laatst een meisje loos* is still sung in the Netherlands. But this is now only a children's song, sung and heard without the awareness that once many maids really fled home to sail the oceans.

Appendix

This is a list of long-term female cross-dressers, listed chronologically by the year of discovery, or the approximate year of occurrence, with the sources and literature, and their male name in quotes.

Note on the abbreviations

    ARA = Algemeen Rijksarchief (General State Archives, The Hague)
    DTB = Doop-, Trouw- en Begraaf Boeken (Baptismal, Marriage and Burial Registers)
    GA = Gemeente Archief (Municipal Archives)
    NA = Notariële Archieven (Notarial Archives)
    RA = Rechterlijk Archief (Judicial Archives)
    VOC-reis = journey from Holland to the East Indies as listed in: *Dutch-Asiatic Shipping in the 17th and 18th centuries*, II, 'Outward-bound Voyages from the Netherlands to Asia and the Cape (1595–1794)', J. R. Bruijn, F. S. Gaastra and I. Schöffer (eds), (Den Haag, 1979).
    WIC = West Indies Company.

1. 1550 Sara Dircxdr., 'Salomon Dircxz'
   GA Amsterdam, RA 567, p. 177v (ed. in: *Vereeniging tot Uitgaaf van het Oud-Vaderlandsche Recht, Verslagen en Mededelingen*, 12 (1960–65), p. 422).
2. 1587 (soldier)
   J. van Beverwijck, *Van de wtnementheyt des vrouwelicken geslachts*, 2 ed (Dordrecht, 1643) II, p. 358.
3. 1589 (soldier)
   Van Beverwijck, *Van de wtnementheyt*, III, p. 51.
   Hugo de Groot, *Annales et historiae de rebus Belgicis* (Amsterdam, 1658) p. 133.
   J. H. Glazemaker, *Toonneel der wereltsche veranderingen* (Amsterdam, 1659) pp. 436–51.
4. 1602 Margarita (soldier)
   C. Ens, *Annalium sive commentarium de bello belgico* (Keulen, 1603–11) VI, p. 203.
   E. van Meteren, *Historiën der Nederlanden* (Amsterdam, 1663) p. 445v.
   De Navorscher, 1858, p. 132.
5. 1606 Maeijken Joosten, 'Pieter Verbrugh', 'Abraham Joosten'.
   GA Leiden, RA 3–6, p. 69v.
6. 1611 Maeyken Blomme (VOC-sailor)
   D. Schoute, *De geneeskunde in den dienst der Oost-Indische Compagnie in Nederlandsch-Indie*, Amsterdam, 1929, p. 33.
7. 1624 Marritgen Pieters
   GA Amsterdam RA 570, f. 79.
8. ca. 1625 Trijntje Sijmons, 'Sijmon Poort' (shoemaker, stonemason, soldier)
   P. de Lange, *Batavise Romeyn* (Amsterdam, 1661) p. 174.

Wonderen des werelds vervattende de uytstekende vreemdigheden en verwonderenswaerdige saken in alderleye gewesten des werelds ontdeckt en voorgevallen (Amsterdam, 1671) p. 62.
9. 1628 Maritgen Jans, 'David Jans' (silk twiner, WIC-soldier)
N. van Wassenaer and B. Lampe, *Historisch verhael alder ghedenckwaerdichste gheschiedenissen*, 21 vols (Amsterdam, 1622–35) year 1629, pp. 57–60.
Van Beverwijck, *Van de wtnementheyt*, II, p. 359.
L. van Zanten, *Spiegel der gedenckweerdighste wonderen en geschiedenissen onses tijds* (Amsterdam, 1661) pp. 337–46.
N. Kluyver, 'Een wonderlijke historie', Eigen Haard (1902) pp. 687–8.
10. 1629 Anna Jans, 'Jan Jansz.' (cook's mate, cook, marine, pikesman in the army)
Van Wassenaer and Lampe, *Historisch verhael*, p. 57.
L. van Zanten, *Spiegel der gedenckweerdighste wonderen*, p. 336.
Wonderen des werelds, p. 62.
11–12. 1629 two women (soldiers)
W. J. Knoop, *Krijgs- en geschiedkundige geschriften*, 8 vols (Schiedam, 1861–7) IV, p. 10.
13. 1632 Barbara Pieters Adriaens, 'Willem Adriaens' (soldier)
GA Amsterdam RA 299, pp. 85v–88; RA 576, sentence 23 October 1632; DTB 439, entry 12 September 1632 (ed. in J. L. van der Gouw, *Oud schrift in Nederland* (Alphen aan den Rijn, 1978, example 19a).
R. B. Evenhuis, *Ook dat was Amsterdam*, II (Amsterdam, 1967) p. 106.
J. ter Gouw, *Amsterdamse kleinigheden* (Amsterdam, 1864) pp. 81–98.
Holland Almanak, 1864, p. 65.
H. O. Feith, 'De strafregtspleging te Groningen, voornamelijk in de zeventiende eeuw', *Bijdragen tot de Geschiedenis en Oudheidkunde inzonderheid van de Provincie Groningen*, 2(1865) pp. 269–301, p. 280.
Magnus Hirschfeld, *Die Transvestiten. Eine Untersuchung über den erotischen Verkleidungstrieb* (Berlin: Pulvermacher, 1910) p. 544.
14. 1641 Vrouwtje Frans (VOC-soldier)
GA Amsterdam RA 304, p. 289: RA 579, 135.
15. 1641 Hendrickgen Lamberts van der Schuyr (soldier)
GA Amsterdam RA 579, p. 113; RA 304, f. 236, 240–3; RA 640-i (II) dossier Willem Willems de Boer; Manuscript Collectie 55, Diary of M. Weveringh, p. 297 (cited in Theo van der Meer, *De wesentlijke sonde van sodomie en andere vuyligheeden. sodomietenvervolgingen in Amsterdam, 1730–1811* (Amsterdam: Tabula, 1984) pp. 138–9).
Koninklijke Bibliotheek, Den Haag, Manuscript 71 J 34, Aernout van Overbeke, Anecdota, no. 278.
Robert James, *Medical dictionary* (London, 1745) III, Chapter 'Tribades'.
Nicolaas Tulp, *Observationum medicarum libri tres* (Amsterdam: Ludovicus Elzevier, 1641) pp. 244–6 (Dutch translation: *De drie boecken der medicijnsche aenmerkingen* (Amstelredam: Jacob Benjamin, 1650) pp. 244–6; also: *Geneeskundige waarnemingen* (Leiden: Juriaan Wishoff, 1740) pp. 330–3.)
F. L. von Neugebauer, *Hermaphroditismus beim Menschen* (Leipzig, 1908) p. 557.
L. S. A. von Römer, 'Der Uranismus in den Niederländen bis zum 19. Jahrhundert', *Jahrbuch für Sexuelle Wissenschaft* 8(1906) pp. 378–9.
L. Faderman, *Surpassing the love of men* (London, 1981) p. 53.

16. 1643 'Claus Bernsen' (VOC-sailor)
J. von der Behr, *Reise nach Java, Vorder-Indien, Persien und Ceylon, 1641–50*, ed. S.P.L. l'Honoré Naber (Den Haag, 1930) pp. 16–17.
17–18. 1644 Hilleke Sell and Jenneke Everts (soldiers)
ARA, Resoluties Raad van State entries 29 February, 11, 12 and 25 March 1644.
19. 1645 'Johannes Kock' (navvy)
GA Amsterdam NA 1074, p. 86, document June 1645; DTB 462, p. 64 (entry 22 April 1645).
20. 1652 'Gerrit Jansz. van Vlissingen' (sailor?)
ARA Admiraliteit van de Maze, Notulen 9 November 1652.
21–25. 1653 Adriana La Noy (sailor)
Jannetje Pieters, 'Jan Pietersse' (sailor)
Aeltje Jans, 'Jan Jansse' (sailor)
Anna Jans (sailor)
Aagt de Tamboer (sailor)
Hollandsche Mercurius, 1653, p. 53 and 69.
De Lange, *Batavise Romeyn*, p. 395.
J. C. de Jonge, *Geschiedenis van het Nederlandsche zeewezen*, 2 vols (Amsterdam, 1858–59) I, p. 507.
J. van Lennep and J. ter Gouw, *De uithangteekens*, 2 vols (Amsterdam, 1868) I, p. 340.
Huisarchief Twickel, 1147, 'minuten van uitgegane stukken van luitenant-admiraal Tromp', 1653.
26. 1653 Anna Alders, alias Wisjewasje
GA Amsterdam RA 309, f. 229v.
27. 1658 Janneken Jans
GA Amsterdam RA 312, f. 155v–156.
28. 1659 Grietje Claas
GA Amsterdam RA 312, f. 214.
29. 1661 Francijntien Theunis 'Jan Theunis'
GA Haarlem, Stad, Burgemeestersnotulen, 15 April 1661.
30. 1663 Annetje Barents, 'Klaas Barends' (pipemaker; VOC-sailor)
Hollandsche Mercurius, 1664, p. 11.
VOC-reis 0997.
31. 1665 Willempje Gerrits (marine)
De Jonge, *Geschiedenis van het Nederlandsche zeewezen*, II, p. 29.
Leven en bedrijf van den vermaarden zeeheld Cornelis Tromp (Amsterdam, 1692) p. 256.
32. 1666 (VOC-sailor or -soldier)
Oprechte Haerlemse Dingsdaegse Courant, no. 23, 8 June 1666.
33. 1666 'Hendrick Albertsz.' (VOC-sailor)
Oprechte Haerlemse Dingsdaegse Courant, no. 23, 8 June 1666.
34. 1667 Engeltje Dirx (VOC-sailor)
GA Amsterdam, RA 317, p. 205.
35. 1667 Jacoba Jacobs, 'Jacob Jacobs' (sailor)
GA Rotterdam, NA 933, p. 103 document 24 March 1667 (ed. in *Rottterdams Jaarboekje*, 1931, p. 68).

C. B. Nicolas, 'Jacoba Jacobs, een marinier van 1665', Marineblad 93(1983) pp. 252–5.
36. 1671 Cornelia Margriete Croon, alias Cornelia Jans
Hans Bontemantel, *De regeeringe van Amsterdam soo in 't civiel als crimineel en militaire (1653–1672)*, G. W. Kernkamp ed., 2 vols ('s Gravenhage: Martinus Nijhoff, 1897) II, p. 286.
GA Amsterdam manuscript 33, f. 281, 281v en 283; RA 320.
GA Groningen, Burgemeesteren en Raad 164, f. 13v, 14 and 22v.
Oprechte Haerlemse Dingsdaegse Courant 26 May and 9 June 1671.
37. 1672 (VOC-soldier)
VOC reis 1211.
38. 1672 Annetje Pieters (sailor)
GA Amsterdam RA 320, f. 83.
39. 1672 Pietertje Pieters
GA Amsterdam RA 320, f. 123v.
40. 1673 Elisabeth Sommuruell (also: Lys St. Mourel), 'Tobias Morello' (soldier, sergeant, drummer)
F. L. Kersteman, *Zeldzaame levensgevallen van J. C. Wyerman*, 2nd edn (Den Haag, 1763), 'Aanhangsel'.
G. J. Rehm, 'Jacob Campo Weyerman en zijn familie', *De Nederlandse Leeuw*, 75(1958) pp. 353–65.
J. P. H. Goossens, 'Nieuwe vragen', *De Brabantsche Leeuw* 3(1954) p. 160.
F. J. G. ten Raa and F. de Bas, *Het Staatsche leger 1568–1795*, VI (Den Haag, 1940) p. 313.
Mededelingen van de Stichting Jacob Campo Weyerman, no. 26 (April 1980) pp. 269–72; 27 (May 1980) pp. 276–8; 40 (June 1981) pp. 414–15.
41. 1673 Isabella Clara Geelvinck (dragoon, cook, valet)
GA Utrecht, Criminele sententien map 1670–84.
Tijdschrift voor de Geschiedenis, Oudheidkunde en Statistiek van Utrecht, 1836, p. 120.
42. 1674 (VOC-soldier)
VOC reis 1274.
43. 1674 Francijntje van Lint (VOC-soldier)
ARA VOC 4011, entry 2 February 1674.
44. 1674 Marrija Margriet Sonnevelt (manservant)
GA Amsterdam RA 322, p. 27v.
45. 1675 Anne Jacobs
GA Harderwijk, Stad 16, p. 21.
J. Schrassert, *Hardevicum antiquum* (Harderwijk, 1732) II, p. 157.
46. 1675 (VOC-soldier)
Dagh-register gehouden in 't casteel Batavia (. . .) Anno 1675, ed. J. A. van der Chijs, ('s Hage: M. Nijhoff, 1902) p. 151, entry 6 June 1675.
47. ca. 1675 (VOC-sailor)
E. C. Godée Molsbergen, *Tijdens de O. I. Compagnie* (Amsterdam, 1932) p. 26.
48. 1677 (VOC-sailor)
VOC-reis 1341.
49. 1679 Trijn Jurriaens, 'Hendrick Brughman'
GA Amsterdam, RA 324, p. 263v; RA 590, p. 177; GA Amsterdam RA 326, p. 263; Particulier Archief 347 (Spinhuis), 39 (Inschrijfboek) p. 28.

Uytertse hylickmaeckers, vol soetigheydt ofte Amsterdamse kermiskoeck (s.a., ca. 1690): 'Van een vrouwmensch dewelke in mansklederen heel treffelijck aengedaen t'Amsterdam in 't spinhuis gebracht is en aldaer moet naeyen en spinnen met een hoed op en broek en wambays aan' (ed. in: Hoefer, *Nederlandsche vrouwen*, p. 67.

50. 1684 Catharin Rosenbrock (sailor and soldier)
    State Archives, Hamburg, Gefangnis 242-1-I, Port C, no. 1, vol. 1, p. 159.
51. 1686 Jannetje Gijsberts de Ridder (VOC-cabinboy)
    ARA VOC 4023, p. 386.
52. 1688 Cornelia Gerritse van Breugel, 'Cornelis Brugh'
    GA Leiden, RA 3–23, p. 5v; RA 10–D, p. 6.
53. ca. 1689 Maria Jacobse de Turenne (soldier)
    GA Den Haag, NA 906, document 1 September 1689 (ed. in: *De Navorscher* N.S. 21(1888) p. 12).
54. 1691 Catarin Fiool,
    GA Amsterdam RA 337, p. 58.
55. 1694 (VOC-sailor)
    VOC reis 1684.
    ARA VOC 1542, p. 281.
56. 1694 Geesje Hooghmeester
    GA Haarlem, Stad, Resoluties van burgemeesters, 31 December 1694.
57. 1696 'Joonas Dirckse' (VOC-sailor)
    ARA VOC 5070, entry 31 March 1696.
58. 1702 Marij Jacobs Weijers (soldier)
    GA Leiden RA 3–28, p. 63v; RA 10-H, p. 80v.
59. 1702 Grietje Harmense Knipsaar, 'Dirk Jansen' (sailor)
    GA Amsterdam RA 351, f. 201; RA 603, p. 225v; RA 604–B, entry 14 July 1702.
60. 1705 Stijntje Barents
    GA Amsterdam RA 354, f. 238v–240v, 241–3, 245v–253; RA 355, f. 16.
61. ca. 1705 Geertruid ter Brugge (dragoon)
    GA Den Haag, DTB 355, p. 322, entry 27 April 1706.
    A. J. Servaas van Rooijen, 'Vrouwen als soldaten', *De Navorscher*, N.S. 21 (1888) p. 12.
62. 1712 (VOC-sailor or soldier)
    ARA VOC 5630, 'Resoluties scheepsraad Arendsduin' 1 May 1712.
63. 1715 (VOC-sailor)
    VOC reis 2251.
    ARA VOC 1873, p. 826 and 922.
64. 1717 (VOC sailor or soldier)
    VOC reis 2301.
    ARA VOC 1888, p. 656.
65–71. 1722 six women (VOC sailors or soldiers)
    F. C. Barchewitz, *Ost-Indianische Reisebeschreibung* (Chemnitz, 1730) p. 609.
72. 1723 Lumke Thoole, alias Johanna Theunis Switters, 'Jan Theunisz' (manservant, VOC-sailor)
    ARA Kaaps Archief 1077, pp. 1014–31.
73. 1725 Maria ter Meetelen (dragoon)
    GA Amsterdam DTB doopboek R. K.-kerk Het Boompje, entry 20 June 1704.
    F. A. Hoefer, *Nederlandsche vrouwen in dienst van Mars* (Rotterdam, 1888) p. 42.

Maria ter Meetelen, *Wonderbaarlyke en merkwaardige gevallen van een twaalfjarige slavernij, van een vrouwspersoon genaemt Maria ter Meetelen, woonagtig tot Medenblik* (Hoorn, 1748) ed. in H. Hardenberg (ed.), *Tussen zeerovers en christenslaven. Noord-afrikaanse reisjournalen* (Leiden, 1950).

74. 1726 Maria Elisabeth Meening (VOC sailor)
    GA Amsterdam, RA Secreet Schepenen Minuutregister, 9 January 1732.
75. 1728 Anna Catharina Hilleghering alias Anna de Moffin alias Dikke Anna
    GA Leiden RA 3–38, p. 27.
76. 1732 (WIC-soldier)
    ARA Archief van de Secretarie van de Gouverneur van Suriname, 1, p. 243.
77. 1732 Lijsbeth Wijngraef, 'Cornelis Wijngraef'
    A. van der Tang, 'Elisabeth Wijngraaff: vrouw of man?', *Scyedam*, 8 (1982) pp. 118–19.
    ARA Hof van Holland 5431.
    ARA RA Brielle 2, sentence 5 July 1694; RA 65 letter 19 March 1695.
    GA Schiedam, stadsarchief 352, entries 2, 7 and 9 October 1694; 40, letter October 1694.
    GA Brielle, stadsarchief, Resoluties Magistraat XX, 10 October 1694.
78. 1735 'Aart den broekman' (farm labourer)
    H. Snellen, *Weezenverpleging bij de Gereformeerden in Nederland tot 1795* (Utrecht, 1915) p. 52.
79. 1743 (stableboy)
    GA Amsterdam, Manuscript B 54, J. Bicker Raye, Notitie van het merkwaardigste meijn bekent, p. 61.
    GA Haarlem, Manuscript II, 5, Jacobus Barnaart jr, Dagverhaal, p. 14.
80. 1743 Maria van der Gijsse, 'Claes van der Gijsse' (soldier)
    Leo Lensen and Willy H. Heitling, *Tussen schandpaal en schavot. Boeven, booswichten, martelaren en hun recht* (Zutphen: Terra, 1985) pp. 135–6.
    Rijksarchief Gelderland, Hof van Gelderland 4604, crimineel proces 1743, no. 2.
81. 1744 (VOC-sailor)
    VOC reis 3314.
82. 1745 Jacobina (VOC-sailor)
    VOC reis 3326.
    ARA VOC 2638, p. 1870.
83. 1745 (VOC-soldier)
    VOC reis 3337.
    ARA VOC 2695, p. 1420.
84. 1746 Johanna Bennius (VOC-sailor)
    VOC reis 3347.
    ARA VOC 2659, p. 1428.
85. 1746 Elisabeth Huyser, 'Jan Drop' (VOC-soldier)
    VOC reis 3379.
    ARA VOC 2686, p. 1006.
86. 1747 (sailor)
    Nederlandsche Jaerboeken 1747, II, p. 767.
87. 1748 Geertruid van Duiren (soldier)
    Rijksarchief Groningen, Staten 183, entry 23 March 1748; 1351, entry 28 March 1748 (ed. in: *Groningsche Volksalmanak* (1899) p. 62).

88. ca. 1750 Maria Sophia Stording (VOC-sailor)
   GA Amsterdam, Bibliotheek J 3-023, Manuscript M. A. Beels, p. 60–B.
89–90. 1751 two women (VOC-soldiers)
   VOC reis 3544.
91. before 1754 Aal de Dragonder (dragoon)
   Z. C. von Uffenbach, *Merkwuerdige Reisen durch Niedersachsen, Holland und Engeland* (Ulm, 1753–4) III, p. 309.
   P. Haverkorn van Rijsewijk, 'Een kijkje op Rotterdam in het begin der achttiende eeuw', *Rotterdams Jaarboekje* (1890) p. 120.
   M. J. van Lieburg, 'Het anatomisch kabinet der clinische school te Rotterdam', *Rotterdams Jaarboekje* (1974) p. 256.
92. 1754 (VOC-soldier)
   VOC reis 3618.
93. 1755 (VOC-sailor)
   VOC reis 3663.
94. 1756 'Jochem Wiesse' (VOC-soldier)
   VOC reis 3680.
   ARA VOC 5265, p. 305; 6341, p. 449v.
95. 1757 (VOC-soldier)
   VOC reis 3697.
96. 1757 (VOC-sailor)
   VOC reis 3711.
97. 1758 (VOC-sailor)
   VOC reis 3728.
98. ca. 1760 Petronella van de Kerkhof (grenadier)
   GA Tilburg, L. D. Lelie, Cronijckje in en ontrent Tilburg voorgevalle (1774–1854) p. 20.
99. 1761 Johanna Elisabeth van Swole, 'Leendert van der Zee' (WIC-soldier)
   ARA Archief van de Societeit van Suriname, 205, p. 183.
100. 1761 Johanna Catharina van Cuijlenberg
   ARA Hof van Holland 5476, no. 8.
101. 1764 'Tiesheld' (VOC-soldier)
   VOC reis 3910.
   ARA VOC 3127, p. 901.
102. 1765 (VOC-sailor)
   GA Amsterdam, Manuscript 55, Diary of M. Weveringh, p. 40.
103. 1768 Marytje van den Hove, 'Alemondus van den Hove'
   GA Alkmaar RA 48–II.
104. 1769 Maria van Antwerpen, 'Jan van Ant', 'Maggiel van Handtwerpen' (soldier)
   Rijksarchief Drenthe, DTB 11, p. 84, entry 21 August 1748.
   Rijksarchief Overijssel, DTB 732, p. 533.
   GA Amsterdam, DTB doopboek R. K. kerk De Posthoorn, entry 15 November 1764; RA 20, pp. 13–15, letter 14 February 1769.
   GA Breda DTB 15, p. 195 entry 17 January 1719.
   GA Gouda, RA 171; RA 181, pp. 64–6.
   Europische Mercurius 72(1751) I, pp. 70–1.
   F. L. K(ersteman), *De Bredasche heldinne, of merkwaardige levensgevallen van Maria van Antwerpen* (Den Haag, 1751) (An annotated edition by Rudolf M.

Dekker, Gert-Jan Johannes and Lotte C. van de Pol is forthcoming).
F. L. Kersteman, *Het leven van F. L. Kersteman*, 2 vols (Amsterdam, 1792) I, p. 102.
'Een vermaekelijk liedeken van een manhaftig vrouwpersoon, die de Staten van Holland vijf jaer en zes maenden gediend heeft als grenadier binnen Breda' in F. A. Hoefer, *Nederlandsche vrouwen*, p. 50 and H. Stalpaert, 'Repertorium van volksliederen op vliegende bladen', *Volkskunde*, 62(1961) pp. 49–92 and 121–56, no. 212.
J. Geselschap, 'Maria van Antwerpen', *Ons Leger* 55(1971) pp. 9–11.
R. M. Dekker and L. C. van de Pol, 'Maria van Antwerpen (1719–1781), een transseksuele vrouw uit de achttiende eeuw?', *Documentatieblad Werkgroep Achttiende Eeuw*, 17(1985) pp. 103–19.

105. 1769 Anna Sophia Spiesen, 'Claas Paulusse' (soldier)
GA Amsterdam RA 431, p. 124.
106. 1769
GA Rotterdam MS 1264 Diary of Jacoba van Tiel, entry 11 May 1769.
107. 1770 Margareta Reymers (VOC-soldier)
ARA VOC 14254, scheepboek Schoonzicht, entry 30 April 1770.
J. S. Stavorinus, *Reize van Zeeland over de Kaap de Goede Hoop naar Batavia*, 2 vols (Leiden, 1793) I, p. 163.
108. 1781 Lena Catherina Wasmoet, 'Claas Waal' (sailor)
GA Amsterdam, RA 447 (1781) p. 503; RA 448, p. 191.
109. 1782 Anna Maria Everts, nicknamed 'de Kwee' (sailor)
ARA RA Zuid-Holland, Crimineele Rol 121, sentence 3 December 1782.
110. 1782 Maria van Spanjen, 'Claas van Vliet', 'Jan Kleyweg', 'Klaas Bly' (sailor, soldier)
GA Rotterdam, RA 35, crimineel examenboek, entry 5 January 1782 (ed. in: Hoefer, *Nederlandsche vrouwen*, pp. 71–7).
111. 1783 Johanna Dorothea Heeght, 'Johannes Hegt' (VOC-sailor)
ARA VOC 4306, p. 385v.
112. 1793 (sailor)
C. De Jong, *Reizen naar Kaap de Goede Hoop, Ierland en Noorwegen, 1791–1797*, 2 vols (Haarlem, 1802–3) II, p. 264.
113. 1794 Johanna van der Meer
GA Leiden RA 3–61, p. 5; RA 10–6, p. 3.
114. 1809 Antje Burger (worker towing barges)
GA's Hertogenbosch, Vonnisboek Hoge Vierschaar 3361B, pp. 113v–115.
115–116. 1810 two women
GA Amsterdam RA 121, p. 6.
117. 1814 Francina Gunningh Sloet, 'Frans Gunningh'
Rijksarchief Gelderland Rechtbank Zutphen sentence 28 December 1814.
Nieuwe Rotterdamsche Courant, 10 February 1924.
Hirschfeld, *Die Transvestiten*, p. 544.
J. W. Staats Evers, *Lijfstraffelijke regtspleging in Gelderland* (Arnhem, D. A. Thieme, 1859) pp. 287–93.
118. 1838 Geertruida Sara Catharina van den Heuvel, 'Jacobus Philippus Vermeijl'
GA Amersfoort, Overlijdensregister, document 22 August 1838 (ed. in: *Het*

Personeelstatuut, Orgaan van de Nederlandse Vereniging van Ambtenaren van de Burgerlijke Stand 30(1979) pp. 7–11).
119. 1839 Johanna Martens (soldier)
Weekblad van het Regt 1 (1839), no. 30, zitting Provinciaal Hof van Holland 7 June 1839.

Notes

Note on the abbreviations:
GA = Gemeente Archief (Municipal Archives)
RA = Rechterlijk Archief (Judicial Archives)
ARA = Algemeen Rijks Archief (General State Archives, The Hague)
VOC = Verenigde Oostindische Compagnie (Dutch East India Company)
WIC = Westindische Compagnie (Dutch West India Company)

CHAPTER 1: INTRODUCTION

1. There is hardly any literature on the subject, with the exception of: F. A. Hoefer, *Nederlandsche vrouwen in dienst van Mars* (Rotterdam: A. Eeltjes, 1888). Several historians have referred to the phenonemon in passing, for example: J. ter Gouw, *Amstelodamiana* (Amsterdam, 1870) I, p. 346; C. Busken Huet, *Het land van Rembrandt* (Haarlem, 1898) II, p. 314; *Maritieme geschiedenis der Nederlanden*, 4 vols (Bussum, 1976–8) II, p. 140; C. R. Boxer, *The Dutch Seaborne Empire, 1600–1800* (Harmondsworth: Penguin Books, 1965) pp. 254–5, who added that in Holland this was more common than in England. The papers of the Hof van Holland (the provincial court of Holland) and the registers of criminal sentences of Leiden are the only series of judicial archives which have been researched completely. Further we have made use of current research projects in judicial archives, such as 'Criminaliteit en Strafrechtstoepassing in de Republiek, in het bijzonder in de achttiende eeuw' (Crime and Criminal Justice during the Republic, especially in the eighteenth century) by H. A. Diederiks, S. Faber and A. H. Huussen, the research of bandits by F. Egmond, and research into the judicial archives of Amsterdam by P. C. Spierenburg, S. Faber, Th. van der Meer, and J. Jüngen. Marine archives proved even less accessible. In *Dutch-Asiatic Shipping in the 17th and 18th Centuries*, II, 'Outward-bound Voyages from the Netherlands to Asia and the Cape (1595–1794)', J. R. Bruijn, F. S. Gaastra and I. Schöffer (eds), (Den Haag, 1979), we found twenty cases of female sailors in the service of the East India Company, although cases were not systematically noted in the research on which this book is based. Archives of the West India Company and of other merchant shipping companies have not been researched. Most of the archives of the navy have been lost. Contemporary literature has not been studied in its totality. Much information and many cases we owe to fellow historians, especially fellow members of the 'Werkgroep Strafrechtgeschiedenis' (Workshop for the study of Crime and Criminal Justice).

2. A Finnish woman in Danish service is mentioned in: *Theatrum Europaeum der wahrhaftige Beschreibung aller denckwürd. Geschichten, 1617–1718* (Frankfurt a.M.: M. Hoffman, 1637–1737) XI, p. 1449. An Italian woman who as a sailor took part in the battle of Lepanto is mentioned in: Colin Thubron, *De*

Venetiaanse vloot (s. l.: *Time Life*, 1981) p. 154. Another Italian case is described in: (Giovanni Bianchi), *Breve Storia della vita di Catterina Vizzani, romana, che per ott'anni vesti abito da uomo in qualita di servidore, la quale dopo vari casi essendo in fine stata uccisa, fu trovata pulcella nella sezzione del suo cadavero* (Venezia: S. Occhi, 1744); This book was translated into English: *(An) Hist(orical) and Physic(al) Dissertation on the Case of Catherine Vizzani, containing the adventures of a young woman (. . .) who for eight years passed in the habit of a man (. . .). With some curious and anatomical remarks on the nature and existence of the hymen (. . .). To which are added certain needful remarks by the English editor* (London: W. Meyer, 1751). On Spain and Portugal see: C. R. Boxer, *Mary and Misogyny. Women in Iberian Expansion Overseas, 1415–1815* (London: Duckworth, 1975) p. 80; The best known Spanish case is Catalina de Erauso, see: Catalina de Erauso, *Historia de la Monja Alferez Dona Catalina de Erauso, escrita por ella misma*, ed. Joaquin Maria de Ferrer (Paris: Julio Didot, 1829). There are several rather well-known French female cross-dressers. See: Ed(ouard) de la Barre – du Parcq, *Histoire militaire des femmes* (Brest: F. Robert, 1873); Ed(ouard) de Beaumont, *L'epée et les femmes* (Paris: Librairie des Bibliophiles, 1881); there is an English translation: *The Sword and Womankind*, ed. Alfred Allinson (London: The Imperial Press, 1905); Adrien Carré, 'Les femmes et la navy du 17e au 19e siècle', in *Neptunia*, 1977, no. 125, p. 33–40 and no. 126, pp. 33–44; John Grand-Carteret, *La femme en culotte* (Paris: Ernst Flammarion, 1899); F. Klein-Rebour, 'Les femmes soldats à travers les ages', *Revue Historique de l'Armée*, 16 (1960) *pp. 3–20*; J. Pichon, *Les femmes soldats* (Limoges: Ussel frères, 1898); C. Romain (= Armand Charmain), *Les guerrières* (Paris: Ed. Berger-Levrault, 1931); Alfred Tranchant and Jules Ladimir, *Les femmes militaires de la France depuis les temps les plus reculés jusque à nos jours* (Paris: Cournol, 1866). Several short articles appeared in: *L'Intermédiaire des chercheurs et des curieux*. The female cross-dressers in France seem to be highly concentrated in the years 1798–1814; see Chapter 3, note 10. It is, however, possible that in France a tradition of female transvestism did exist more similar to the Dutch and English tradition than appears from the literature mentioned above. This is suggested by some cases found during a research of eighteenth-century Parisian Judicial Archives by Arlette Farge. See Arlette Farge, *La vie fragile. Violence, pouvoirs et solidarités à Paris au XVIIIe siècle* (Paris: Hachette, 1986) p. 182. In France there also appeared several contemporary (auto) biographies: [Jean de Préchac], *L'Heroine mousquetaire, histoire veritable* (Paris, 1713; reprinted, for example, Bruxelles: P. Witte, 1722); translated into Dutch as *De Musket-Draagende Heldin, ofte een Waarachtig Verhaal van het Doorluchtige Leeven (. . .) van Kristina van Meirak* (Amsterdam: T. ten Hoorn, 1679) and reprinted in 1680, 1686, 1739, 1760. Translated into English as *The Heroine Musqueteer, or the Female Warrior: a True History* (London: J. Orme for J. Wellington, 1700). Of the following book we found only the title of a translation mentioned in *Notes and Queries*, 6e S, III, p. 113: *The Female Warrior: a True History, very delightful and full of pleasant Adventures in the Campaigns of 1676 and 1677, Translated from the French* (London, 1678). See also Chapter 5 note 41. A very exceptional case was that of the Chevalier d'Eon, an obscure member of the French eighteenth-century diplomatic circles, who for long periods dressed as a woman. His behaviour aroused

much attention in the press. He must be mentioned here because in his time it was widely believed that his true sex was female. See Michel de Decker, *Madam Le Chevalier d'Eon* (Paris: Perris, 1987).
3. As in the Netherlands, historians have noted, but not systematically researched, and always underestimated the phenomenon. The military historian John W. Fortescue estimated the number of female soldiers to be sixteen (cited in Elisabeth Ewing, *Women in Uniform through the Centuries*, (Totowa, N.J.: Rowman & Littlefield) p. 28; The marine historian Peter Kemp wrote that there had been only very few female sailors; see: *The British Sailor: a Social History of the Lower Deck* (London, 1970) p. 490. A few cases from the middle of the seventeenth century are described in Antonia Fraser, *The Weaker Vessel: Women's Lot in Seventeenth Century England* (London: Weidenfeld & Nicolson, 1984) pp. 196–201. In older historical studies female cross-dressers are mainly viewed as human curiosities: Robert J. Blackman, *Woman: In Honour and Dishonour* (London: Sampson Low, Marston & Co., 1920); O(scar) P(aul) Gilbert, *Women in Men's Guise* (London: John Lane, 1932) translated from the French; Francis Gribble, *Women in War* (London: Sampson Low, Marston & Co., 1916); Reginald Hargreaves, *Women-at-Arms: Their Famous Exploits Throughout the Ages* (London: Hutchinson & Co., 1930); Bram Stoker, *Famous Impostors* (New York: Sturgis & Walton, 1910); C.J.S. Thompson, *Mysteries of Sex: Women Who Posed as Men and Men Who Impersonated Women* (London:Hutchinson & Co., 1938); J. David Truby, *Women at War: A Deadly Species* (Boulder, Co.: Paladin Press, 1976). See also Chapter 5 notes 39 and 44. Several cases have been found in journals like *Notes and Queries* and *The Mariner's Mirror*. They have not been researched systematically. A quick look through *The Annual Register* yielded cases of female cross-dressing in 1761 (p. 149 and 170), 1766 (p. 116), 1769 (p. 148), 1771 (p. 71), 1773 (p. 111), 1777 (pp. 191–2), 1782 (p. 221), 1793 (p. 19), and 1807 (p. 496). Very recently, the subject has begun to draw attention from feminist historians. See for example Lynn Friedli, 'Women who dressed as men' in *Trouble and Strife*, 6(1985) pp. 25–9; There are also current research projects by Anna Clark and Julie Wheelwright. In England too several (auto) biographies of female cross-dressers were published in the seventeenth, eighteenth and the beginning of the nineteenth centuries. See: Memie Muriel Dowie, *Women Adventurers: the Lives of Madame Velazquez, Hannah Snell, Mary-Anne Talbot, and Miss Christian Davies* (London: T. Fisher Unwin, 1893); William Fairbank, *The Surprising Life and Adventures of M(aria) Knowles* (New Castle, c.1805) (reprinted in J. Ashton, *Eighteenth Century Waifs* (London: Hurst & Blackett, 1887) pp. 191–4.); Anne Jane Thornton, *Interesting Life and wonderful Adventures of A. J. Thornton, the Female Sailor (. . .). Written by herself* (London: 1835). See also Chapter 3, notes 14, 20, 23 and 39. We found two Dutch books which are translated from the English, but of which the original could not be found: *De Berugte Land – en Zeeheldin, of de Wonderbare Levensgevallen van Anne Blound, anders Robert Stafford* (Amsterdam: Steven van Esveld, 1756); [Henriette de Boston], *Nieuwe Zee – en Landreize in 't Jaar 1726 gedaan door Mejuffrouw Henriette de Boston, Door haarzelfs in 't Engelsch beschreeven* (Amsterdam: Jan Roman en Steeve van Esveldt, 1735).

American cases are described in Jonathan Katz, *Gay American History:*

Lesbians and Gay Men in the U.S.A. (New York: Thomas Y. Cromwell Co., 1976); in the United States also (auto) biographies of female cross-dressers appeared: [Herman Mann], *The Female Review: Life of Deborah Sampson, the Female Soldier in the War of the Revolution* (New York: Arno Press, 1972) (first edn 1797); *The Female Marine or Adventures of Miss Lucy West*, ed. Alexander Medlicott jr, (New York: Da Capo Press, 1966) (reprint of the edition of 1817), which is probably fictional; The following also may be fictitious: Loreta Janeta Velazquez, *The Woman in Battle; A Narrative of the Exploits, Adventures, and Travels of Madame Loreta Janetta Velazquez, Otherwise Known as Lieutenant Harry T. Buford, Confederate States Army*, ed. C.J. Worthington (New York: Arno Press, 1972) (first edn: Hartford: T. Belknap, 1876).
4. C. A. Davids, *Wat lijdt den zeeman al verdriet: Het Nederlandse zeemanslied in de zeiltijd (1600–1900)* (Den Haag: Martinus Nijhoff, 1980) pp. 92–3.
5. The 119 cases of cross-dressing have been listed chronologically in the Appendix. Here the sources for every case are included; the women who are named throughout this book can be looked up there via the index.

CHAPTER 2: WOMEN WHO LIVED AS MEN

1. *Het Wonderlik Leven En de Oorlogsdaaden, Van de Kloekmoedige Land en Zee Heldin. Waarachtige geschiedenis*, Wiel Kusters (ed.), 2 vols (Maastricht: Scorpio, 1982), first edn: Amsterdam: Jacobus en Jan Bouman, 1706, reprinted in 1720).
2. Natalie Zemon Davis, 'Women on top' in Id., *Society and Culture in Early Modern France* (Stanford: California University Press, 1975) pp. 124–52, reprinted with some changes and with the sub-title 'Symbolic Sexual Inversion and Political Disorder in Early Modern Europe' in Barbara A. Babcock (ed.), *The Reversible World: Symbolic Inversion in Art and Society* (Ithaca-London. Cornell University Press, 1978) pp. 147–93. See also Chapter 5, note 37.
3. GA Amsterdam RA 453, 382–7, 411, 422 and 443, entry 13 July 1784 (Anna de Jager).
4. J. Wagenaar, *Vaderlandsche historie*, 21 vols (Amsterdam, 1752–59) XX, pp. 90–1. Cf. R. M. Dekker, 'Women in Revolt: Popular Protest and Its Social Basis in Holland in the 17th and 18th centuries', *Theory and Society*, 16 (1987) pp. 337–62.
5. GA Gorinchem, manuscript 3; On the relation between male transvestism and riots, see Davis, 'Women on top'; Yves-Marie Bercé, *Fête et révolte. Des mentalités populaires du XVIe au XVIIIe siècle* (Paris: Hachette, 1976) pp. 83–6; Malcolm I. Thomis and Jennifer Grimmett, *Women in protest 1800–1850* (London: Croom Helm, 1982).
6. H. E. van Gelder, *'s Gravenhage in zeven eeuwen* (Amsterdam: Meulenhoff, 1937) p. 151. Cf. J. ter Gouw, *De volksvermaken* (s.a., s.l.) p. 673.
7. 'Vrouwen in manskleederen op de kermis te Delfshaven in 1694', *Rotterdamsch Jaarboekje*, 5 (1896) pp. 85–8.
8. GA Amsterdam RA 596, f.48v, 6 June 1689 (Lijsbet Hendriks).
9. *Journaal van Constantijn Huygens den Zoon*, I (Utrecht, 1876) p. 380, entry 25 December 1690. Cf. the case of a gentleman from Groningen, travelling with

a valet who was rumoured to be a girl: J. A. Worp, 'Gerard Nicolaas Heerkens', *Groningsche Volksalmanak*, 1899, pp. 1–51, p. 19. Cf. N. de Roever, *Uit onze oude Amstelstad* (Amsterdam: Minerva, s.a.) p. 81.
10. GA Amsterdam RA 451, pp. 297–300 and 303, entry 8 March 1783 (Johanna Pikhof and Adam Kitter).
11. ARA Hof van Holland 5509–2.
12. H. O. Feith, 'De strafregtspleging te Groningen, voornamelijk in de zeventiende eeuw', *Bijdragen tot de Geschiedenis en Oudheidkunde inzonderheid van de Provincie Groningen*, 2 (1865) pp. 269–301, p. 280.
13. P. Haverkorn van Rijsewijk, *De oude Rotterdamsche Schouwburg aan de Coolsingel* (Rotterdam, 1882) pp. 119–20. Cf. H. C. H. Moquette, *De vrouw*, 2 vols (Amsterdam: H. Meulenhoff, 1915) II, p. 69.
14. S. Hart, *Geschrift en getal* (Dordrecht, 1976) pp. 115–83.
15. Marina Warner suggested that illegitimate birth was a common background for cases of cross-dressing but our findings do not prove this hypothesis. See Marina Warner, *Joan of Arc. The Image of Female Heroism* (Harmondsworth: Penguin Books, 1983) p. 161.
16. Brigitte Eriksson (ed.), 'A Lesbian Execution in Germany, 1721: the Trial Records', *Journal of Homosexuality*, 6(1980–81) pp. 27–41, p. 33. The German text was reprinted in Ilse Kokula (ed.), *Weibliche Homosexualität um 1900 in zeitgenössischen Dokumenten* (München: Frauenoffensive, 1981) pp. 91–112.
17. Julie Wheelwright, unpublished paper, and 'Amazons and Military Maids', *Women's Studies International Forum*, 10(1987) pp. 489–502.
18. D. F. Scheurleer, *Van varen en van vechten*, 3 vols ('s Gravenhage: Martinus Nijhoff, 1914), 'Een nieuw lied op een Vrouwe Matroos', III, pp. 572–4.
19. Cf. Davis, 'Women on Top'.
20. Cf. Chapter 1, note 4.
21. The same holds for Antoinette de Bourignon: Antoinette de Bourignon, *Het leven van juffr. Antoinette de Bourignon* (Amsterdam: Jan Rieuwertsz. and Pieter Arentz., 1683) pp. 18–19.
22. Paul Andersen and Deborah Cadbury, *Imagined Worlds* (London: BBC, 1985) p. 21.
23. *Mariner's Mirror*, 4(1913) p. 92.
24. Kersteman, *De Bredasche Heldine*, pp. 118–19 and 124.

CHAPTER 3: MOTIVES AND TRADITION

1. Kersteman, *Bredasche heldinne*, pp. 2, 4, 5, 7, 9, 10, 17, 71, 89, 104, 105, 114; trial record.
2. *De grootmoedige en heldhaftige Hollandsche amasoon* (Den Haag: Joh. Meusert, 1775) p. 4. Travelling by women in men's clothes is mentioned as a matter of course in N. Camstrup, *Rampspoedige reysbeschryving ofte journaal van 's ed. Oostindische Compagnies schip Blydorp* (Amsterdam, 1735) p. 10.
3. *Maritieme Geschiedenis der Nederlanden*, V (Bussum: De Boer Maritiem, 1977) p. 166.
4. *Algemene Geschiedenis der Nederlanden*, V (Bussum: Unieboek, 1980) p. 154.
5. *Dutch-Asiatic Shipping, passim*; A literary rendering of this theme is to be found

in: Gerrit van Spaan, *De gelukzoeker overzee, of de Afrikaansche wegwijzer*, (Rotterdam: Pieter de Vries, 1752) p. 309.
6. Philologus Philiatros a Ganda (= Jacobus van de Vivere), *De wintersche avonden of Nederlantsche vertellingen* (Amsterdam, 1615) p. 119.
7. Ivan Illich, *Gender* (New York: Pantheon Books, 1982) pp. 143–5.
8. Hugo de Groot, *Annales et historiae de rebus Belgicis* (Amsterdam, 1658) p. 133.
9. Gerda H. Kurtz, *Kenu Symonsdochter van Haerlem* (Assen: Van Gorcum, 1956).
10. Jeanne Bouvier, *Les femmes pendant la Révolution de 1789* (Paris: E. Figuière, 1931); Raoul Brice, *La femme et les armées de la Révolution et de l'Empire 1792–1815 D'après des mémoires, correspondances et documents inédits* (Paris: L'Edition Moderne, 1913); Emile Cère, *Madame Sans-Gêne et les femmes soldats 1792–1815* (3rd edn Paris: Plon, 1894); F. Gerbaux, 'Les femmes soldats pendant la Révolution', *La Révolution française*, 47 (1904) pp. 47–61; Adrien Lasserre, *La participation collective des femmes à la Révolution française: Les antécedents du féminisme*, (Paris, 1906) pp. 323–40. On the counter-revolutionary side women also fought; two of these published autobiographies: (Renée Bordereau, dite Langevin), *Mémoires de Renée Bordereau, dite Langevin, traitant sa vie militaire dans la Vendée* (Paris: L. G. Michaud, 1814) (translated in Dutch as: *Geschiedenis van Renée Bordereau genoemd Langevin betrekkelyk haar militaire leven in de Vendée, opgesteld door haar zelve. Uit het Fransch vertaald* (Dordrecht: A. Blussé en zoon, 1815); Françoise Després, *Détails historiques sur les services de Françoise Després, employée dans les armées royales de la Vendée depuis 1793 jusqu'en 1815 (...) écrits par elle-même* (Paris: L. G. Michaud, 1817).
11. Ralph Pettow, *Der krankhafte Verkleidungstrieb. Beiträge zur Erforschung der Travestie* (Pfullingen in Württemberg: Johannes Baum Verlag, 1922); cf. 'Frauen als Soldaten im Weltkriege', Vierteljahrsberichte des Wissenschaftlich-humanitären Komités während der Kriegszeit, herausgegeben statt der Jahrbuch für Sexuelle Zwischenstufen, I (April 1915) pp. 36–48; II (July 1915) pp. 95–8; III (October 1915) pp. 120–48.
12. Scheurleer, *Van varen*, III, p. 205.
13. *Reisen van Nicolaus de Graaff*, J. C. M. Warnsink (ed.) ('s Gravenhage, 1930) pp. 19–22.
14. [Mary Ann Talbot], *The Life and Surprising Adventures of Mary Anne Talbot in the Name of John Taylor, a Natural Daughter of the Late Earl Talbot (...). Related by Herself* (London: R. S. Kirby, 1809). This was reprinted several times, see for example: Dowie, *Women Adventurers*, pp. 135–96, p. 196.
15. For example Hillegond Engels van Velsen (GA Amsterdam RA 350, f. 43v–44; RA 604 B, entry 24 February 1701).
16. Anton Blok, 'De rol van vilders in de Bokkenrijders-benden', *Volkskundig Bulletin*, 7(1981) pp. 121–43.
17. E. J. Hobsbawm, *Bandits* (Harmondsworth: Penguin Books, 1972), Appendix: Women and banditry; Carsten Küther, *Räuber und Gauner in Deutschland. Das organisierte Bandenwesen im 18. und 19. Jahrhundert* (Göttingen: Vandenhoeck und Ruprecht, 1976) pp. 84–5.
18. GA Amsterdam RA 371, f. 117v–122v, 150 and 153, entry 8 January 1715 (Anne Marie Piernau). GA Amsterdam RA 348, p. 183, 15 November 1699 (Lystet Jacobs de Bruyn).
19. GA Amsterdam RA 371, f. 36, 52v–53, 75v and 82v, entry 8 November 1714 (Eytje Hendriksz).

20. [Mary Frith], *The life and death of Mrs. M. F., commonly called Mal Cut-purse (. . .)*, (London, 1662); T. Middleton and T. Dekker, *The Roaring Girl*. The Tudor Facsimile Texts (s.l., 1914) (first printed 1611). Cf. *Dictionary of National Biography*, XX (London, 1889) pp. 280–1.
21. Lotte C. van de Pol, 'The Image and Reality of Prostitution in the Dutch Republic' in C. Brown (ed.), *Images of the World: Dutch Genre Painting in Its Historical Context*, forthcoming; Id., 'Van speelhuis naar bordeel? Veranderingen in de organisatie van de prostitutie te Amsterdam in de 18e eeuw', *Documentatieblad Werkgroep Achttiende Eeuw*, 17(1985) pp. 103–19.
22. Lotte van de Pol, 'Vrouwencriminaliteit in de Gouden Eeuw', *Ons Amsterdam*, 34(1982) pp. 266–9; an extensive study is in preparation.
23. Kersteman, *Bredasche Heldinne*, p. 9; [Daniel Defoe], *A General History of the Pyrates*, Manuel Schonhorn (ed.) (London: J. M. Dent & sons, 1972) p. 155 (first printed 1724; Dutch translation: *Historie der Engelsche zeerovers* (Amsterdam, 1725).
24. (F. L. Kersteman), *Zeldzaame levensgevallen van J. C. Weyerman* ('s Gravenhage: Pieter van Os, 1763).
25. Eriksson (ed.), *A Lesbian Execution*, p. 33.
26. Sherry B. Ortner and Harriet Whitehead (eds), *Sexual Meanings: the Cultural Construction of Gender and Sexuality* (Cambridge University Press, 1981); Shirley Ardener (ed.), *Defining Females: the Nature of Women in Society* (London: Croom Helm, 1978); Karen Hastrup, 'The Sexual Boundary: Transvestism and Homosexuality', and 'The Sexual Boundary: Purity, Virginity and Heterosexuality', *Journal of the Anthropological Society of Oxford*, 5, no. 3 (1974) pp. 137–47, and 6, no. 1(1975) pp. 42–56; Mary Douglas, 'The Two Bodies' in idem, *Natural Symbols: Explorations in Cosmology* (London: Barrie & Jenkins 1971) pp. 93–112; Mary Douglas, *Purity and Danger* (London: Routledge & Kegan Paul, 1966).
27. See for example: Gisela Bleibtreu-Ehrenberg, *Der Weibmann: Kultische Geschlechtswechsel im Shamanismus: Eine Studie zur Transvestition und Transsexualität bei Naturvölkern* (Frankfurt a.M.: Fisher, 1984); Hermann Baumann, *Das doppelte Geschlecht. Ethnologische Studien zur Bisexualität in Ritus und Mythos* (Berlin: Dietrich Reimer, 1955).
28. Charles Callender and Lee M. Kochems, 'The North American Berdache', *Current Anthropology*, 24(1983) pp. 443–56; Evelyn Blackwood, 'Sexuality and Gender in Certain Native American Tribes: the Case of Cross-Gender Females', *Signs*, 10(1984) pp. 27–43.
29. James M. Freeman, *Untouchable: an Indian life history* (Stanford University Press, 1979) *passim*; Unni Wikan, 'Man Becomes Woman: Transsexualism in Oman as a Key to Gender Roles', *Man*, N.S. 12(1977) pp. 304–19.
30. Hélène d'Almeida-Topor, *Les Amazones: Une armée de femmes dans l'Afrique précoloniale* (Paris: Rochevigne, 1984).
31. Elisabeth Tietmeyer, *Frauen heiraten Frauen. Eine vergleichende Studie zur Gynaegamie in Afrika* (Hohenschäftlarn: Renner Verlag, 1985).
32. René J. M. Grémaux, 'Neither Male nor Female: Sworn Virginity in the Balkans (19th–20th Century)', unpublished paper, 1985. A dissertation is in preparation.
33. Erich Seemann, 'Die Gestalt des kriegerischen Mädchens in den europäischen Volksballaden', *Rheinischen Jahrbuch für Volkskunde*, 10(1959) pp. 192–212.

34. Stith Thompson, *Motif-Index of Folk-Literature: a Classification of Narrative Elements in Folktales, Ballads, Myths, Fables, Mediaeval Romances, Exempla, Fabliaux, Jest-Books, and Local Legends*, 6 vols (Copenhagen: Rosenkilde and Bagger). These themes are respectively: D513.1, K1321, F565.1.3, K1837.4, K1236, K1837.8 and H1578. Cf. Pierre Samuel, *Amazones, guerrières et gaillardes* (Grenoble: Complexe-Presses Universitaires de Grenoble, 1975).
35. *Handwörterbuch des deutschen Märchens*, I (Berlin: Walter de Gruyter, 1930–33) p. 92; Johannes Bolte en Georg Polivka, *Anmerkungen zu den Kinder-u[nd] Hausmärchen der Brüder Grimm*, II (Hildesheim: Georg Olms, 1963) pp. 56–60.
36. Warner, *Joan of Arc*, pp. 146–63.
37. Theo van der Meer, *De wesentlijke sonde van sodomie en andere vuyligheeden. Sodomietenvervolgingen in Amsterdam 1730–1811* (Amsterdam: Tabula, 1984) p. 111.
38. Kurtz, *Kenu*, pp. 77–81.
39. See note 20; Henry Fielding, *The Female Husband, or the Surprising History of Mrs. Mary Alias Mr. George Hamilton, Who Was Convicted of Having Married a Young Woman of Wells (. . .)*, (1746), repr. edn Claude E. Jones (Liverpool University Press, 1960) pp. 29–51. See on this work: Sheridan Baker, 'Henry Fielding's The Female Husband: Fact and Fiction', *Publications of the Modern Language Association of America*, 74(1959) pp. 213–24, p. 224.
40. Pettow, *Verkleidungstrieb*, pp. 22–3; The source he gives, namely Karl Braun, *Blütiger Blätter. Erzählungen*. (Breslau: Schnottländer, 1883) could not be traced by us.
41. Cf. note 25.
42. John Anson, 'The female transvestite in early monasticism', *Viator*, 5(1974) pp. 1–32; Vern L. Bullough, 'Transvestism in the Middle Ages', *American Journal of Sociology*, 79(1974) pp. 1381–94 (repr. in: Vern L. Bullough and James Brundage (eds), *Sexual Practices and the Medieval Church* (Buffalo N.Y.: Prometheus Books, 1982) pp. 43–54); Marie Delcourt, 'Le complexe de Diane dans l'hagiographie chrétienne', *Revue d'Histoire des Religions*, 153(1958) pp. 1–33; Evelyn Patlagean, 'L'histoire de la femme déguisée en moine et l'évolution de la sainteté féminine à Byzance', *Studi Medievali*, 3rd Series 17(1976) II, pp. 598–623.
43. Jean-Claude Schmitt, *Le Saint Lévrier. Guinefort, guérisseur d'enfants depuis le XIIIe siècle* (Paris: Flammarion, 1979) p. 159. Cf. Jacques Dalarun, *Robert d'Arbrissel, fondateur de Fontevraud* (Paris: Albin Michel, 1986) p. 132.
44. Warner, *Joan of Arc*, pp. 146–63.
45. Antoinette de Bourignon, *Het leven van juffr. Antoinette de Bourignon*, pp. 18–19.

CHAPTER 4: SEXUALITY

1. J. M. W. van Ussel, *Geschiedenis van het seksuele probleem* (Meppel: Boom, 1972).
2. Lawrence Stone, *The Family, Sex and Marriage in England 1500–1800* (London: Weidenfeld & Nicolson, 1977).

3. Vern L. Bullough, *Sexual Variance in Society and History* (University of Chicago Press, 1976).
4. Peter Laslett, *Family Life and Illicit Love in Earlier Generations: Essays in Historical Sociology* (Cambridge, 1977).
5. J.-L. Flandrin, *Familles: Parenté, maison, sexualité dans l'ancienne société* (Paris, 1976), and Idem, *Le sexe et l'occident. Evolution des attitudes et des comportements* (Paris, 1981); G. R. Quaife, *Wanton Wenches and Wayward Wives: Peasants and Illicit Sex in Early Seventeenth Century England* (London, 1979); cf. Philippe Ariès and André Béjin (eds), *Western Sexuality: Practice and Precept in Past and Present Times* (Oxford: Basil Blackwell, 1985).
6. Edward Shorter, *The Making of the Modern Family* (New York: Basic Books, 1977).
7. For the Netherlands: Donald Haks, *Huwelijk en gezin in Holland in de 17de en 18de eeuw. Processtukken en moralisten over aspecten van het laat 17de en 18de eeuwse gezinsleven* (Assen: Van Gorcum, 1982); 'De sexualiteit in de achttiende eeuw', Special issue of the *Documentatieblad Werkgroep Achttiende Eeuw* 17(1985); Herman W. Roodenburg 'The Autobiography of Isabella de Moerloose: Sex, Childrearing and Popular Belief in Seventeenth Century Holland', *Journal of Social History* 18(1985) pp. 517–39; Rudolf Dekker and Herman Roodenburg, 'Humor in de zeventiende eeuw. Opvoeding, huwelijk en seksualiteit in de moppen van Aernout van Overbeke (1632–1674)', *Tijdschrift voor Sociale Geschiedenis*, 10(1984) pp. 243–67.
8. *Herculine Barbin dite Alexina B.*, with a preface by Michel Foucault (Paris: Gallimard, 1978); N. O. Body, *Aus eines Mannes Mädchenjahren*, with a preface by Rudolf Presber, and a conclusion by Magnus Hirschfeld (Berlin: Hesperus Verlag, s.a.)
9. Examples of fairs can be found in diaries, for example J. Bicker Raye, Notitie van het merkwaardigste meijn bekent, p. 55, manuscript GA Amsterdam, ms.B 54 (Amsterdam); *Journaal van Constantijn Huygens den Zoon*, II, p. 142, entry 4 November 1692 (Gravesend, England); Provinciale Bibliotheek Friesland, O.F.R., Reis van een Leeuwarder in Nederland en Duitschland (1752) pp. 9–10 (Kleve, Germany). Many medical books from the 17th and 18th centuries have a chapter on hermaphrodites, like J. V. E. (= Venette), *Venus minsieke gasthuis* (Amsterdam, 1695) pp. 584–610. Cf. Dorothy Price, 'Mammalian Conception, Sex Differentiation, and Hermaphroditism as Viewed in Historical Perspective', *American Zoologist*, 12 (1972) pp. 179–91; Franz Ludwig von Neugebauer, *Hermaphroditismus beim Menschen* (Leipzig: Dr Werner Klinkhardt, 1908).
10. Magnus Hirschfeld, *Die Transvestiten. Eine Untersuchung über den erotischen Verkleidungstrieb* (Berlin: Pulvermacher, 1910). Cf. Peter Ackroyd, *Dressing Up. Transvestism and Drag, the History of an Obsession* (London: Thames & Hudson, 1979). Also: Mieke de Waal, *Vriendinnen onder elkaar: Travestieten en transsexuelen in Nederland* (Amsterdam, De Arbeiders pers, 1982).
11. GA Breda, RA vonnisboek 113, entry 17 March 1711 GA Amsterdam RA 352, f. 107v (Jan Snoeck); GA Amsterdam, RA 631 (Moses Gerrits).
12. On the history of homosexuality, see: Vern L. Bullough, *Homosexuality: a history* (New York: New American Library, 1979); 'Historical Perspectives on Homosexuality', Special issue of the *Journal of Homosexuality*, 6 (1980/1)

no. 1/2; Alan Bray, *Homosexuality in Renaissance England* (London: Gay Men's Press, 1982). For the Netherlands, see: Van der Meer, *De wesentlijke sonde van sodomie*; Theo van der Meer, 'Legislation against sodomy and persecution of sodomites in the Dutch Republic in the 18th century: the acknowledgement of an identity', Paper presented at the conference 'Sex and the State', University of Toronto, Toronto, Canada, 3–6 July 1985. A special issue of the *Journal of Homosexuality* is forthcoming with contributions on the Netherlands by L. J. Boon, G. Hekma Th. van der Meer and others.

13. It is significant that the word *tribadie* is not to be found in the *Woordenboek der Nederlandse Taal*, the most complete and authoritative dictionary of the Dutch language.
14. Judith C. Brown, *Immodest Acts: the Life of a Lesbian Nun in Renaissance Italy* (New York: Oxford University Press, 1986) p. 6.
15. Lillian Faderman, *Surpassing the Love of Men: Romantic Friendship and Love Between Women from the Renaissance to the Present* (New York: William Morrow, 1981); P. J. Buynsters, *Wolff en Deken, een biografie* (Leiden: Martinus Nijhoff, 1984).
16. Brown *Immodest Acts*, pp. 17–19.
17. Van der Meer, *Wesentlijke sonde*, p. 169; Arend H. Huussen jr., 'Sodomy in the Dutch Republic During the Eighteenth Century', *Eighteenth Century Life*, 9(1985) pp. 169–78. Cf. Bray, *Homosexuality*, p. 86.
18. ARA 2e Afd. Nationaal Gerechtshof 185 (Woudrigem).
19. Harry Benjamin, *The Transsexual Phenomenon* (New York, 1977, first impr. 1966); Vern L. Bullough, 'Transsexualism in History' in *Archives of Sex Behavior* 4(1975) pp. 561–71, reprinted in: Id., *Sex, Society, and History* (New York: Science History Publications, 1976, pp. 150–161); Richard Green, 'Mythological, Historical and Cross-Cultural Aspects of Transsexualism' in Richard Green and John Money (eds), *Transsexualism and Sex Reassignment* (Baltimore: Johns Hopkins University Press, 1969) pp. 13–22; Leslie Martin Lothstein, *Female-to-Male Transsexualism: Historical, Clinical, and Theoretical Issues* (Boston: Routledge & Kegan Paul, 1983).
20. Kersteman, *De Bredasche Heldinne*, p. 71.
21. Robert Jesse Stoller, *Splitting: a Case of Female Masculinity* (New York, 1974).
22. Theo van der Meer, 'Liefkozeryen en vuyligheeden', *Groniek*, 12(1980) no. 66, pp. 34–7.
23. Gudrun Schwarz, 'Mannweiber in Männertheorien' in Karin Hausen (ed.), *Frauen suchen ihre Geschichte* (München: Beck, 1983) pp. 62–80; Cf. George Chauncey jr, 'From Sexual Inversion to Homosexuality: Medicine and the Changing Conceptualization of Female Deviance', *Salmagundi*, 58–9(1982/3), pp. 115–46. George Chauncey jr, 'Christian Brotherhood or Sexual Perversion? Homosexual Identities and the Construction of Sexual Boundaries in the World War One Era', *Journal of Social History*, 19(1985) pp. 189–213. Esther Newton, 'The Mythic Mannish Lesbian: Redclyffe Hall and the New Woman' in *The Lesbian Issue: Essays from Signs* (University of Chicago Press, 1985), pp. 7–27.

CHAPTER 5: CONDEMNATION AND PRAISE

1. On Amsterdam see Sjoerd Faber, *Strafrechtspleging en criminaliteit te Amsterdam, 1680–1811: De nieuwe menslievendheid?* (Arnhem: Gouda Quint, 1983);

Cf. Pieter Spierenburg, *The Spectacle of Suffering. Executions and the Evolution of Repression: from a Preindustrial Metropolis to the European Experience* (Cambridge University Press, 1984).
2. Cf. Chapter 2, note 3 (Anna de Jager).
3. Cf. Chapter 3, note 15 (Hillegond Engels).
4. Cf. Chapter 2, note 10 (Johanna Pikhof and Adam Kitter).
5. Van der Meer, *Wesentlijke sonde*, pp. 36–49; Jean Papon, *Receuil d'arrests notables des cours souveraines de France* (Geneva, 1622) pp. 1257–8.
6. Pieter Spierenburg, *Judicial Violence in the Dutch Republic; Corporal Punishment, Excutions and Torture in Amsterdam, 1650–1750* (Universiteit van Amsterdam, 1978).
7. Rudolf Dekker and Lotte C. van de Pol, 'Wat hoort men niet al vreemde dingen...', *Spiegel Historiael*, 17 (1982) pp. 486–94; Fred Martin, 'De liedjeszanger als massamedium: Straatzangers in de achttiende en negentiende eeuw', *Tijdschrift voor Geschiedenis*, 97(1984) pp. 422–47.
8. Scheurleer, *Van varen*, III, p. 351; R. F. Rammelman, 'Matroosliedere op die Kaapvaart in die 17e en 18e eeu', *Kwartaalblad van die Suid-Afrikaanse Bibliotheek*, 15(1961) pp. 12–17, p. 14.
9. J. van Lennep, *Zeemanswoordenboek* (Amsterdam, 1856) p. 75.
10. 'Een nieuw aerdigh liedeken van Monsr. Splitruyter, die haer eenige jaren, in manskleedinge op sijn frans gekleet heeft onthouden en onder-trout is geraeckt met seker juffrou binnen Amsterdam, en daerover aldaer in 't Tuchthuys sit en te sien is in 't selve habijt' in *Uytertse Hylickmaeckers vol soetigheydt ofte Amsterdamse Kermis-koeck* (Amsterdam: Cloppenburg, ca. 1690) pp. 65–6.
11. 'Een nieuw liedt van twee vrouwluyden die t'samen getrout zijn in de Nieuwe Kerck tot Amsterdam' in *Den Italiaenschen Quacksalver ofte den Nieuwe Amsterdamsche Jan Potazy* (Amsterdam: Wed. G. de Groot, 1708) pp. 71–3.
12. Hoefer, *Nederlandsche vrouwen*, pp. 66–9.
13. *Uytertse hylickmakers*, pp. 66–8.
14. Hoefer, *Nederlandsche vrouwen*, pp. 49–50.
15. Scheurleer, *Van varen*, III, p. 582.
16. Hoefer, *Nederlandsche vrouwen*, p. 57.
17. Ibid., pp. 53–4.
18. Fridericus Spanheimius, *De papa foemina inter Leonem IV et Benedictum III: Disquisitio historica* (Leiden: Johannes Verbessel, 1691).
19. *Europische Mercurius*, 1749, I, p. 20.
20. *Europische Mercurius*, 1727, I, p. 94.
21. Fr. Esauz, *Christelick tresoirtjen* (Amsterdam, 1645) p. 60.
22. Philologus Philiatros a Ganda (=Jacobus van de Vivere), *Avonden*, p. 119.
23. Simon de Vries, *D'eedelste tijdkorting der weetgierige verstanden of de groote historische rariteitenkamer* (Amsterdam, 1682) I, p. 119.
24. Koninklijke Bibliotheek Den Haag, ms, 71 J 34, Arnout van Overbeke, *Anecdote*, no. 278, cited in: Dekker en Roodenburg, *Humor in de zeventiende eeuw*, p. 261.
25. Wiel Kusters, 'Over het aantrekken van een broek', *De Revisor*, 5(1978) pp. 50–5. This count is based on M. Buisman, *Populaire prozaschrijvers van 1600 tot 1815* (Amsterdam, 1959). The oldest travesty novel dates from 1624: E. K. Grootes *et al.* (eds), *Wonderlicke avontuer van twee goelieven* (Muiderberg: Coutinho, 1984).

26. *De bagijn in mansklederen* (Amsterdam: Phil. Verbeek, 1706).
27. A. G. l. m., *De wonderlijke reisgevallen van Maria Kinkons. Behelzende in zig haare geboorte, de geheime vlugt van haar ouders, haar ontmoetingen onder een mannelijk gewaad, zo te land als te zee enz.* (Harlingen: Bouwe Schiere, 1759).
28. P. J. Buynsters, 'Petrus Lievens Kersteman, een achttiende eeuwse romanschrijver' in H. Heestermans (ed.), *Opstellen door vrienden en vakgenoten aangeboden aan C. H. A. Kruyskamp* ('s Gravenhage, 1977) pp. 29–41.
29. See for titles: Chapter 1, notes 2 and 3, Chapter 3 notes 10 and 23, Chapter 5 note 36. For Germany, see Jeanine Blackwell, 'An Island of Her Own: Heroines of the German Robinsonades from 1720 to 1800', *The German Quarterly*, 58(1985) pp. 5–26. Also: Estelle Jelinek, 'Disguise Autobiographies: 'Women Masquerading as Men', *Women's Studies International Forum*, 10(1987) pp. 53–62.
30. Alfred Holtmont, *Die Hosenrolle. Das Weib als Man* (München: Jessen Verlag, 1925); cf. Simon Shepherd, *Amazons and Warrior Women. Varieties of Feminism in Seventeenth Century Drama* (Brighton: Harvester Press, 1981); Melveena McKendrick, *Woman and Society in the Spanish Drama of the Golden Age: a Study of the Mujer Varonil* (Cambridge University Press, 1974).
31. C. Huygens' *Trijntje Cornelisdr.*, ed. H. J. Eymael (Zutphen: W. J. Thieme, s.a.), p. 57. Cf. Jacobus van Vergelo, *De Kryghsgesinde dochter* (Dendermonde: Jacobus J. Ducau, ca 1735) first edn 1670. Kenau Simons Hasselaar was made the heroine of several plays: Steven van der Lust, *Herstelde hongersdwangh* (Haarlem: Korn. Themisz. Kas, 1660); Willem Hessen, *Beleegering van Haarlem* (Haarlem: Iz. van Hulkenroy, 1739) (first edn 1689).
32. John Harold Wilson, *All the King's Ladies: Actresses of the Restoration* (University of Chicago Press, 1958) p. 73.
33. *Biographie Universelle*, XVII (Paris: L. G. Michaud, 1820) pp. 537–38 (Maupin); *Dictionary of National Biography*, X (London: Smith, Elder & Co., 1887) pp. 65–7 (Charke); See Chapter 2, note 13.
34. See Chapter 2, note 3 and Chapter 3, note 20 and Chapter 5 note 38. Kathleen Crawford, *The Transvestite Heroine in Seventeenth-Century Popular Literature* (Harvard University Press, 1984) could not be obtained by the authors.
35. Taco K. Looijen, *Ieder is hier vervuld van zijn voordeel. Amsterdam in de ogen van buitenlanders* (Amsterdam: Peter van der Velden, 1981) p. 65.
36. (Hannah Snell), *The Female Soldier; or the Surprising Life and Adventures of Hannah Snell* (London: R. Walker, 1750). Repr. Dowie, pp. 57–181. Dutch translation: *De vrouwelyke soldaat of de verbazende levensgevallen van Anna Snel* (Amsterdam: Gerrit de Groot, 1750). This autobiography is based upon reality, see S. Monnier, 'Travestie in de populaire literatuur in de achttiende eeuw', unpublished paper, 1979, Documentatiecentrum Nederlandse Literatuur, Universiteit van Amsterdam; Cf. *Dictionary of National Biography*, LIII (1898) pp. 205–6.
37. David Kunzle, 'World Upside Down: The Iconography of a European Broadsheet Type', in Babcock (ed.), *Reversible World*, pp. 39–95. Many Dutch prints are reproduced in F. van Veen, *Dutch Catch Penny Prints: Three Centuries of Pictural Broadsides for Children* (The Hague: Van Hoeven, 1971). See further on the theme of cross-dressing: Davis, 'Women on top'; Jean Delumeau, *Le pèche et la peur: La culpabilisation en Occident (XVIIe–XVIIIe*

siècles) (Paris: Fayard, 1983), p. 143-53; Bob Scribner, 'Reformation, Carnival and the World turned Upside-down, *Social History*, 3(1978) pp. 303-29; Peter Burke, *Popular Culture in Early Modern Europe* (New York: Haper & Row, 1978) pp. 185-91. Cf. Chapter 2, note 2.

38. Boxer, *Mary and Misogyny*, p. 80; *Enciclopedia Universal Ilustrada Europeo-Americana*, XX (Bilbao: Espasa-Calpa, s.a.) pp. 412-13; Emile Laurent, 'Psychologie feminine. Catalino de Erause, la Monja Alferez', *Archives d'Anthropologie Criminelle*, 24(1909) pp. 508-13. See also Chapter 1, note 2.

39. Ellen C. Clayton, *Female warriors: Memorials of Female Valour and Heroism, from the Mythological Ages to the Present Era*, 2 vols (London: Tinsley Bros., 1879), II, p. 23 etc.; *The Life and Adventures of Mrs. Christian Davies commonly called Mother Ross, who, in several campaigns under King William and the late Duke of Marlborough in the quality of a foot soldier and dragoon gave many signal proofs of an unparallell'd courage and personal bravery, Taken from her own mouth when a pensioner of Chelsea-Hospital* (London: R. Montagu, 1740); several times reprinted, see also: Dowie, *Women adventurers* pp. 199-288, p. 179.

40. *Museum des buitengewonen en wondervollen behelzende ware gebeurtenissen uit onzen tijd* (Amsterdam: C. L. Schleijer, 1820) pp. 14-29.

41. [L. van den Bosch], *Derde vervolg van saken van staat en oorlog in en omtrent de Vereenigde Nederlanden (. . .) 1692-1697* (Amsterdam, 1699), book 24, p. 125. *Histoire de la dragone, contenant les actions militaire et les adventures de Geneviève Prémoy, sous le nom du Chevalier Balthazar* (Brussels, 1703; repr. 1721).

42. 'Vrouwen als soldaten', *Nederlandse Spectator*, 17 October 1885, p. 343; Cf. Brice, *La femme et les armées*, p. 342.

43. *Kloekmoedige Land en Zee Heldin*, II, pp. 42-4.

44. *Theatrum Europaeum* XV, p. 77; John Laffin, *Women in Battle* (London: Abelard-Schuman, 1967) p. 26, cf. p. 21.

45. P. J. Meertens Instituut, Amsterdam, Volksliedarchief.

CHAPTER 6: SOME CONCLUSIONS

1. Aletta H. Jacobs, *Herinneringen* (Amsterdam: Van Holkema en Warendorf, 1924) p. 14.

2. Late examples are: Isobel Rae, *The Strange Story of Dr. James Barry, Army Surgeon, Inspector-General of Hospitals Discovered on death to be a Woman* (London: Longman, Green & Co., 1958). Andrew Barrow, *Gossip: History of High Society from 1920 to 1970* (London: Pan Books, 1978) pp. 43-4, on 'Colonel Barker'.

3. A. Pitlo, *De zeventiende en achttiende eeuwsche notarisboeken en wat zij ons omtrent ons oude notariaat leeren* (Haarlem: H. D. Tjeenk Willink, 1948) p. 272.

4. 'Female Warriors' in *The works of Oliver Goldsmith*, ed. J. W.M. Gibbs, 5 vols, I (London: George Bell & Sons, 1908) pp. 315-20. This work is probably not by Goldsmith.

5. *Nieuwe reize van Misson na en door Italien (. . .) vermeerdert (. . .) van Addisson*, 2 vols (Utrecht: Willem van de Water en Jacob van Poolsum, 1724) I, p. 318.

6. Anke Pouw, 'De "Waare Verlichting" van de vrouw. Vrouwen en gezin binnen het burgerlijk beschavingideaal van de Maatschappij tot Nut van't Algemeen. 1784-c.1840', *Comenius*, September 1986.

Index

The index includes the permanent Dutch cross-dressers, alphabetically listed by their first name. The number after the name refers to the list of names in the appendix. Some names occur in the sources in different forms, so note that, e.g. Johanna = Jannetje = Jaantje, Elisabeth = Lysbeth, and Maria = Maritgen = Marretje = Marytje.

Aagt de Tamboer (21–5), 83
Aal de Dragonder (91), 73
'Aart den broekman' (78), 82
Addison, John, 100
Adriana La Noy (21–5), 18
Aeltje Jans (21–5), 81
Africa, 92
   Nuer 42, 92
   Dahomey, 41–2
   Cape of Good Hope, 19, 28–9, 73, 77
   see also Maritgen Jans
Amazons, xv, 90
Anna Alders (26), 32, 36, 39
Anna Catharina Hilleghering (75), 35
Anna Jans (10), 11, 22
Anna Maria Everts (109), 44, 50
Anna Sophia Spiesen (105), 14, 29
Anne Jacobs (45), 50
Annetje Barents (30), 14, 22

Balkans, 42, 44–5
Barbara Pieters Adriaens (13), 11, 13–14, 19, 60–2, 80, 82–3, 86, 89, 91
Barbin, Hercule, 50
Barchewitz, 19
Benjamin, Harry, 64
berdache, 41
Berg, Antoinette, German cross-dresser, 96
'Hendrik van den Berg', *see* 'Stout-Hearted Heroine'
Beverwijk, Johannes van, 90
Bible, condemnation of transvestism in the, 45, 75, 91
Blound, Anne, English cross-dresser, 93
Bokkenrijders band, 35
Bordereau, Renée, French cross-dresser, 93
Boston, Henriette de, English cross-dresser, 93
Bougainville, 23
Bourignon, Antoinette de, 46
Brielle, 51–2
Brown, Judith, 57

Bruyn, Mietje de, 8
Bunkens, Isabe, German cross-dresser, 44
Bullough, Vern, 47

Catharin Rosenbrock (50), 19, 23
Catharijn Fiool (54), 36
Cauldwell, D., 64
Charke, Charlotte, 94
'Claus Bernsen' (16), 22
Coevorden, 65
Cornelia Gerritse van Breugel (52), 58, 60, 63, 80, 86–7
Cornelia Margriete Croon (36), 37
'Cornelius, Robert', English cross-dresser, 96
cross-dressing, *see* transvestism

'Davies, Christian', (Mother Ross) English cross-dresser, 16, 96
Deeken, Aagje, 58
Delft, 7, 13
Denmark, 1, 5

East Indies, 14, 19, 27–9, 33–4
East Indies Company, *see* VOC
Elisabeth Sommuruell (40), 36, 40, 96
Engeltje Dirx (34), 28
England, 1, 2, 16, 35, 38, 44, 91, 93–4, 96, 102
   London, 94
   Anne, Queen of, 96
   Stadhouder Willem III, as King of, 96
   George IV, King of, 96
Ens, Caspar, 91
Erauso, Catalina de, Spanish cross-dresser, 94, 96

Faderman, Lillian, 57
Flandrin, Jean-Louis, 47–8
France, 31, 89, 93–4, 96, 102
   Lyon, 91
   Paris, 8, 39

126

Index

Francijntje van Lint (43), 73
Francina Gunningh Sloet (117), 11, 36, 39, 62, 70, 102
Frith, Mary, (Moll Cutpurse), English cross-dresser, 38, 44, 94

Geertruid ter Brugge (61), 94
Geertruida Sara Catharina van den Heuvel (118), 15, 20, 82
Germany, 1-2, 8, 10, 16, 37, 40, 44, 50-1, 95-6
Emden, 5, 29
Halberstadt, 40
Hamburg, 23, 37
Oldenburg, 12
Prussia, the King of, 96
Gorinchem, 7
Gouda, *see* Maria Van Antwerpen
Gouw, Jan ter, 61
Graaff, Nicolaus de, 34, 80, 92
Grietje Claas (28), 33, 39
Groningen, 19, 37, 62, 83
Groot, Hugo de, 31

The Hague, 7, 51, 87, 94
Hamilton, Mary, English cross-dresser, 44
Harderwijk, 50
Hasselaar, Kenau Simons, 31, 44
Hendrickgen Lamberts van der Schuyr (15), 52, 58, 79, 83, 91
hermaphroditism, see (pseudo-)hermaphroditism
Hessel, Phoebe, English cross-dresser, 96
Hirschfeld, Magnus, 54
homosexuality, (female), 55-63, 69-72
and law, 70, 77-80
Huygens, Constantijn jr, 8

intersexuality, 49-53
Isabella Clara Geelvinck (41), 19-20, 36-7
Italy, 1, 57, 93

Jacoba Jacobs (35), 14
Jacobs, Aletta, 99
Jannetje Gijsberts de Ridder (51), 29
Jannetje Pieters (21-5), 22, 81
Joan of Arc, 43, 90
Joan, Pope, 90, 94
Johanna Catharina van Cuijlenberg (100), 30
Johanna Martens (119), 29, 36
Johanna van der Meer (113), 39, 54

'Johannes Kock' (19), 60
'Joonas Dirckse' (57), 22

Lena Catharina Wasmoet (108), 14, 20, 83
Lumke Thoole (72), 29, 50-1, 77
Lijsbeth (Elisabeth) Wijngraef (77), 51, 58
Kersteman, Franciscus Lievans, 4, 93
Lange, Pieter de, 90
Laslett, Peter, 47
Leiden, 9, 59
Lincken, Catharina, German cross-dresser, 16, 40, 44
Lothstein, Leslie, Martin, 69

Maeyken Blomme (6), 28
Maeyken Joosten (5), 59, 79-80
maling, 61, 83
Margareta Reymers (107), 39
Margarita (4), 30, 83
Maria van Antwerpen (104), 1, 3-4, 11, 14-19, 23-7, 40, 44, 63-9, 78-9, 82-4, 86, 89, 92-3, 96-7
Maria Elisabeth Meening (74), 28, 81
Maria van der Gijsse (80), 14, 20, 32, 76
Maria ter Meetelen (73), 27, 92
Maria van Spanjen (110), 13, 19, 22, 30, 77
Maritgen Jans (9), 11, 13, 15-16, 18-21, 33, 81-2, 91
marriage of two women, 58-63, 91
Marritgen Pieters (7), 54
Marytje van den Hove (103), 12, 14, 35, 50
Maupin, Madame de, 94
Meirak, Christine de, French cross-dresser, 93
menstruation, 15
Middelburg, 28
migration, 10-11, 33-4
Mother Ross, *see* Christian Davies

Napoleon, 96
Neugebauer, Franz Ludwig, 52

Papon, Jean, 78
Pettow, Ralph, 31
Prémoy, Géneviève, French cross-dresser, 93, 96
prostitutes and prostitution, 8, 26, 36, 39, 41, 48, 54
(pseudo-)hermaphroditism, 49-51
Quaife, G. R., 47

Read, Mary, English cross-dresser, 40
Rees, 73
Rotterdam, 73, 75, 77
Russia, Tsar of, 96

saints, 44–6
Schellinck, Maria, Flemish cross-dresser, 96
Schiedam, 51–2
sexuality, 16, 21, 47–73, 87–8
  history of, 47–8
sex-test, 43
Shorter, Edward, 48
Sinistrati, Luigi Maria, 63
Snell, Hannah, English cross-dresser, 93–5
songs, 2, 16–17, 33, 39, 83–90, 97
sorcery, 44
Southern Netherlands, 10, 88, 96–7
Spain, 1, 27, 93–4, 96
  Philips IV, King of, 96
Spanheim, Frederic, 90
Stoller, Robert, 68
Stone, Lawrence, 47
'Stout-Hearted Heroine of the Land and the Sea', 5–6, 21, 93, 96
Stijntje Barents (60), 36, 39
suicide, 23

Tahiti, 23
Talbot, Mary Ann, English cross-dresser, 35, 96
Texel, 11
theatre, 6, 8, 55, 94, *see also* transvestism in plays
Thompson, Stith, 43
transsexuality, 63–9
transvestism, female
  temporary, 6–8
  during Carnival, 7
  during travel, 8, 27
  during war, 30–2
  in folklore, 7
  as erotic device, 8
  and law, 75–80
  in novels, 92–5
  in plays, 94
  in prints, 94–5
  and crime, 35–9
  motives for, 25–46
  as medical term in modern psychology, 53–5

transvestism, male, 54–5
transvestites, female
  origins and youth, 10–13
  work, 9
  transformation 13–17
  impersonation, 17–19
  discovery of, 19–24
  looks, 16–17
  professions, 9–10
  anonymous Dutch female transvestites, (32), 29, (46), 29, (79), 22, 93, (86), 36, (102), 23, (106), 75
tribady, *see* female homosexuality
Tromp, Cornelis, 80
Trijn Jurriaens (49), 20, 37–8, 77, 87
Trijntje Sijmons (8), 10, 14, 73
Tulp, Nicolaas, 52, 56, 92

Utrecht, 13, 20, 37

virgins, virginity, 44–6, 90
Vivere, Jacobus van de, 31, 91
Vizzani, Catarina, Italian cross-dresser, 93
VOC (Dutch East Indies Company), 2, 9, 16, 19, 27–8, 34, 81, 103
Vries, Simon de, 91
Vrouwtje Frans (14), 14

Warner, Marina, 43
Wassenaer, Nicolaas van, 91
Westphal, Carl von, 71
WIC (Dutch West Indies Company), 9, 18, 21, 81
Willem III of Orange, Stadhouder, 8, 96–7
Willem IV of Orange, Stadhouder, 97
Willempje Gerrits (31), 5–6, 96
Witsen, Nicolaas, xv
Wolff, Betje, 58

Zwolle, 62, 66